Entrepreneurial you

MONETIZE YOUR EXPERTISE
CREATE MULTIPLE INCOME STREAMS
AND THRIVE

Entrepreneurial
you

DORIE CLARK

HARVARD BUSINESS REVIEW PRESS

Boston, Massachusetts

The web addresses referenced in this book were live and correct at the time of the book's publication but may be subject to change.

Library of Congress Cataloging-in-Publication Data

Names: Clark, Dorie, author.
Title: Entrepreneurial you : monetize your expertise, create multiple income streams, and thrive / by Dorie Clark.
Description: Boston, Massachusetts : Harvard Business Review Press, [2017]
Identifiers: LCCN 2017012025 | ISBN 9781633692275 (hardcover : alk. paper)
Subjects: LCSH: Entrepreneurship. | Career development. | Expertise—Economic aspects.
Classification: LCC HB615.C647 2017 | DDC 650.1—dc23 LC record available at https://lccn.loc.gov/2017012025

The paper used in this publication meets the requirements of the American National Standard for Permanence of Paper for Publications and Documents in Libraries and Archives Z39.48-1992.

ISBN 9781633692275
eISBN 9781633692282

To Ann Thomas and Gail Clark,
with love and gratitude

CONTENTS

Why I Wrote This Book

It's the dirty secret of today's entrepreneurial economy: being excellent, and even being well known and respected in your field, just isn't enough.

The internet and our globalized economy have given us the possibility of reaching millions of people, working on our own terms, and enjoying unlimited income potential. But for too many professionals, that's just not been the reality. Instead, we live in a world where "success" has increasingly been decoupled from income. In the course of my travels, I've run across way too many top-notch professionals who are excellent at what they do, yet struggle to earn what they're worth. You can be talented and well regarded, but unless you're very deliberate about the choices you make, you may end up earning little for your efforts.

What went wrong? And how can we reverse that negative trend and reap the potent promise of entrepreneurship?

To answer those questions, I interviewed more than fifty successful entrepreneurs, earning high six-, seven-, and eight-figure incomes with solo or very small businesses. This book distills the secrets I learned—practical hands-on advice about how to monetize your expertise and build a sustainable, thriving business in the new economy.

Whether you're an entrepreneur, an aspiring entrepreneur, or an employed professional seeking to maximize your options, you'll find in these pages proven strategies that will help you develop new income streams that leverage the work you're already doing, and open up new opportunities for freedom and flexibility.

The path that led me to write this book started in 2006 when I launched my own marketing strategy consulting business after working previously as a journalist, presidential campaign spokesperson, and nonprofit executive director.

In the early days, I was just happy to be working for myself, from home. My sole focus then was bringing in revenue and getting my business solvent; I took on clients of almost any size for projects of almost any scope. There was the speech I wrote for a nonprofit chairman for $500, the $1,000 communications plan for a government agency, and the multiple times I flew across the country to do weekend-long trainings for $600 plus airfare (my client was so cheap that on one trip, I had two connections each way). It wasn't pretty.

I spent the first years of my business hustling fanatically, working long hours, networking face to face in search of business and directly servicing clients on site. As I built my business into a more sustainable venture, I eventually cut out the hundred-dollar projects, and within a couple of years, I was earning a healthy, six-figure income.

But most days I was still stuck in client meetings or driving hours to get to them. I found myself in a common trap for successful entrepreneurs: you've built up a business so robust that you don't have time to do anything but service your existing clients.

I knew that if I kept on the same path, I could continue to grow my business over the years and have a perfectly nice quality of life. In time, I'd go from being thought of as a "talented, rising young consultant" to being the go-to consultant in my market, and I might even land some of the local blue-chip firms as clients.

But I wanted more than that.

I was frustrated that I couldn't travel as much as I wanted for pleasure, because I was locked down by client meetings and the expectation (which I'd helped to cultivate) that I'd always be on call. Even though I worked for myself, I didn't feel particularly free.

I wanted to accomplish two things: to upgrade the clients I worked with to larger companies with bigger budgets; and to extricate myself from the ongoing press of day-to-day client responsibilities and develop a more location-independent business model.

Getting there wouldn't be simple. It's easy to step to the next branch if it's right in front of you. But I had to take a leap of faith. My business to that point had been traditional marketing consulting for local companies with which I had some kind of personal connection, whether direct or through a referral.

I knew it would be very difficult to move beyond that—to jump into a new echelon of elite clients—by moving incrementally along the existing path. I needed to do something different to attract positive attention from people I didn't already know, to reinvent myself and change my positioning in the marketplace.

To learn how to do that, I interviewed dozens of professionals who had successfully changed jobs or careers or how they were perceived by others. In 2013, that work led to my first published book, *Reinventing You*, which shares best practices in personal branding and professional reinvention, and answers the question: *How can you make big changes, and position yourself for the career you want?* The book is essentially a road map to help professionals make the transitions they seek.

But once you shift into your desired field, I realized, there's another problem to solve: *How can you work your way to the top and ensure that others recognize your expertise?*

That was the question I sought to answer in *Stand Out*, my second book. I interviewed many of the world's top experts, including business luminaries like Seth Godin, David Allen, Robert Cialdini, Tom Peters, and more, to understand how they developed breakthrough ideas and built a following around them. In that book, I laid out a blueprint for how regular professionals can follow those same principles to ensure their own talents get noticed.

As I soon learned, however, becoming a recognized expert these days doesn't always lead to money. The elephant in the room of modern entrepreneurship is that even people who seem to be at the top of their game aren't always monetizing successfully. Learning to make money from your expertise is *a different skill set* from what's needed to become excellent at your work or well known in your field (two critically important things that I cover in depth in *Reinventing You* and *Stand Out*, but that aren't, on their own, sufficient for big earnings).

That's why I conceived of these three books as a trilogy, with *Entrepreneurial You* as the logical and essential conclusion. *Entrepreneurial You* seeks to address what I believe is the most important question of all: *How can you create a long-term, sustainable business that rewards you emotionally, intellectually, and financially?*

I want to see more talented people sharing their ideas in the world. But that won't be possible until they're able to create lasting, successful careers for themselves. With this book, I share ideas, strategies, and best practices for monetization that I hope make it more likely for everyone to succeed.

I try to practice what I preach. I learned an enormous amount from the entrepreneurs and "side hustlers" profiled in this book. The year I spent writing *Entrepreneurial You* has been my most lucrative to date, as a direct result of implementing the techniques I share in this book. I grew my income by more than $200,000 that year, and I continue to experiment with new strategies and channels. Successful entrepreneurship should be thought of as an ongoing pilot, not a finished state.

The changes I've made have allowed me to create the business I want today, where I live in New York City (but could live anywhere if I chose) and travel frequently to interesting destinations for work (I wrote the first draft of this prologue on a flight to Aspen, and the final draft on a flight back from Amsterdam).

My current business model—fueled by seven distinct income streams—didn't just happen. It was a series of conscious and deliberate choices. I hope that by sharing what I've learned from the exceptionally successful entrepreneurs profiled in this book, and by recounting a bit of my own journey along the way, you'll be able to make your own informed choices about what you'd like your business model—and your life—to look like, and shape it accordingly. Let's get started.

PART ONE

Build Your Brand

CHAPTER 1

The Entrepreneurial Opportunity

I had made it. I was flying back from Asia in a business-class seat, stretched out and sipping a complimentary mimosa. I'd just earned $35,000 for two weeks of teaching at a university overseas. It was intensive—six hours in front of the classroom each day, all while fighting a bad cold. But the amount I earned in those two weeks nearly equaled *my entire year's salary* before starting my own business, as a marketing-strategy consultant, in 2006.

In the intervening decade, I'd discovered that entrepreneurship suited me. Within a year of launching my business, I was feeling fulfilled and earning six figures advising interesting clients like Google, Yale University, and the US National Park Service. Since then, I'd been growing my business slowly and steadily—my own vision of the good life.

But shortly after I walked off that flight from Asia, I received an email that made me wonder how well I was really doing after all. It was from my friend John Corcoran, an attorney and blogger in the San Francisco Bay Area who'd immersed himself over the past several years in online marketing. A few times a week, he'd send out helpful articles and other content to his email list, which I always enjoyed receiving.

That month, however, he'd also been promoting two digital courses created by some well-known leaders in the online marketing world. Corcoran had signed up as an "affiliate," and if his readers made a purchase, he'd get a commission. Affiliate marketing is a win-win, bringing in new customers and rewarding the person who does so at no cost to the customer. I had emailed him before my flight to find out how his promotion was going.

"I ended up converting 32 buyers," he wrote me. "That's about $28K in revenue for five or six emails, one blog post, and one video throughout the month. If I add in other blog- and podcast-related income, I probably earned about $33–34K related to my blog alone last month."

My jaw dropped. He added: "I didn't work any more hours last month than I did in previous months."

I had always thought of online marketing as something vaguely scammy—the world of Nigerian princes and spam emails hawking discounted Viagra. "MAKE MONEY ONLINE!" their messages would scream—and I'd hit delete. I'd written it off completely.

But Corcoran made me realize I'd been missing something huge. Online marketing done right didn't have to be exploitive or crass. And it could provide something powerful that I'd been lacking: a way to increase and diversify my revenue and minimize risk in my income stream. Yes, I was already working with multiple clients and doing various kinds of work—consulting, speaking, executive coaching, and business school teaching. But now I saw that I still wasn't diversified *enough*.

Most entrepreneurs focus too much on earning revenue from one or two activities (such as consulting and speaking) and overlook other opportunities that can help free them from trading time for dollars. Diversifying can simultaneously enable you to earn more and mitigate risk.

What's more, the opportunity isn't just for entrepreneurs: even if you currently work for an organization full time and have no desire to become self-employed, developing entrepreneurial pursuits on the side can provide an additional income stream, as well as unexpected professional development opportunities.

Lenny Achan began his career as a nurse and worked his way up to becoming an administrator at Mount Sinai Hospital in New York City. But his career really took off when his supervisor discovered Achan had developed an app on the side. Achan was worried when he got called into his boss's office: *Had he violated a policy he hadn't known about? Did they suspect he had been moonlighting on company time?* As it turned out, his boss admired his initiative and promoted him to run social media—and eventually all communications—for the hospital.

Similarly, Bozi Dar—who was born in Serbia and now lives in the United States—has a traditionally successful career as a senior marketing executive for a *Fortune* 500 life sciences company.[1] But he became fascinated by the possibilities of entrepreneurship, and in 2013, he also tried to build an app, which ended up costing him $45,000 in development fees. It never earned a profit, but he learned invaluable lessons in the process about marketing, sales, and business strategy. The next year, he tried a different tack: an online course about how to get promoted at your company.

Dar's course has been far more successful than his app, earning him $25,000 in its first year alone. But he's actually seen some of the biggest returns in his day job, where he says his ability to bring a background in "technology and digital is highly desirable. It enabled me to completely reinvent myself." He considers himself an "intrapreneur," innovating inside his company, and he feels that continuing to operate in a large corporate environment, with its teams and budgetary resources, allows him to tackle "high-profile ideas that would be incredibly hard to work on as an entrepreneur." (You can read more about Dar's story and learn his tips for identifying your areas of expertise in the sidebar "Assessing Your Areas of Expertise," at the end of chapter 2.)

Whether we work for ourselves or for others, we all need to find ways to diversify our revenue streams. That allows us to hedge against uncertainty, increase our impact, and earn more.

In my previous books, *Reinventing You* and *Stand Out*, I focused on how to develop your personal brand and ensure your expertise is recognized in the marketplace. Now in *Entrepreneurial You*, I'll do what other recent books on career development don't: I'll show you *how to make money* in the uneasy economic environment in which we find ourselves today and create multiple, sustainable sources of income.

Many of the entrepreneurs profiled in this book work in the realm of marketing, leadership, and communications. That's the world I know best, and one that I believe is at the leading edge when it comes to reinventing career paths and creating new strategies for monetization. But there are also plenty of case studies here featuring talented entrepreneurs in food, fashion, personal finance, and more. Regardless of your field, the foundational principles I share apply broadly; my goal is for you to see yourself and find new possibilities in the stories, whatever your current field or profession. Please note that unless otherwise specified, all quotes in the book come from personal interviews I conducted.

Additionally, many of the case studies, especially later in the book, focus on online marketing. That's by design. Not everyone needs to become an online entrepreneur, and the early chapters of this book focus on decidedly analog activities like consulting, coaching, and professional speaking.

In much of *Entrepreneurial You*, however, you'll find a heavy dose of information about internet-based techniques—from podcasting to blogging to online communities. That's because these are newer paths to monetization and therefore often the ones that talented professionals haven't yet explored or mastered. Even if you're not planning on diving into the online world yet, these techniques are worth learning about so you have more options for the future.

Whether you're a dedicated entrepreneur, a full- or part-time freelancer, or are hatching a sideline apart from your corporate job (and possibly planning your transition out of that job altogether), my hope and intention is for these pages to provide a blueprint for monetizing your expertise, both online and off.

It's all about learning how to amp up the earning potential of a "portfolio career."

Why We All Need Portfolio Careers

Common wisdom tells us that we should diversify our investment portfolios because it's foolish to put all our money in one stock. But we're far less careful on the other end. Too many of us rely on one employer for our entire sustenance, just as I once did.

Nearly fifteen years before that fateful flight back from Asia, I was fresh out of grad school and working as a political reporter at a weekly newspaper. Late one Monday afternoon, the human resources director called me into his office; I thought perhaps they were changing our dental plan. Instead, I got laid off, effective immediately—an early victim of the collapsing news-paper industry. HR gave me a box to pack up my desk and one week's severance pay. I had no idea how I was going to support myself. I had to move fast.

The next morning—September 11, 2001—I woke up and flipped on the television. The day I needed to start looking for a job was the day America changed forever. Planes stopped flying, the stock market stopped trading, and absolutely no one wanted to hire an out-of-work reporter.

That's when I started to understand the precarious nature of relying on one revenue stream; it could all be taken away instantly. For months, I tried to get another job in journalism, but no one was hiring. I scraped by freelancing; in a good week, I could pull down $800, but more often I brought in half that amount. Finally, I landed a full-time job as the spokesperson on a gubernatorial campaign; I earned what felt like a princely $3,000 per month, until we lost in the primary. I freelanced for another six months until getting hired as the spokesperson on a presidential campaign, which we also lost.

No job, I realized, is secure. Yet working without a "guar-anteed" salary still seemed frightening to me; I saw a lot more risks than opportunities. By then I'd run out of choices, however, so I unwillingly became part of the vanguard of entrepreneurs developing a portfolio career—piecing together freelance work and ultimately starting my own business with various revenue streams.

Today, after more than a decade as an entrepreneur, my opin-ion has reversed. I now believe it's far riskier *not* to be diversi-fied; if you're relying on one paycheck from one employer, you may be courting disaster. The old model, the one that most of us grew up hearing about—"work hard, get a good job, and you'll be rewarded"—has changed. Hard work is still mandatory, but today, the work has shifted toward an ever more independent, work-from-wherever-you-are business economy. The very idea of what constitutes a career has transformed.

Why? Because technology and the global economy, among other forces, have triggered monumental changes in the world of work that will continue to multiply in the future. When I started my first job at the Boston weekly newspaper, I thought I'd be a journalist for the rest of my life. Back in 2000, newspapers were still extremely lucrative; they were rolling in advertising revenue. The online world was such a minor consideration that our newsroom made do with only one internet-connected computer. I had signed on to the industry at the exact moment it started its inexorable collapse, but I couldn't see it at the time. When it comes to identifying the precise tipping point of future trends, I doubt any of us can.

In recent years, technology-induced disruption has crushed a number of once-stalwart brands, from Circuit City to Blockbuster to Borders. Plus, there are a lot fewer jobs to go around these days. From 1948 to 2000, jobs grew 1.7 times faster than the population.[2] But from 2000 to 2014, the population grew 2.4 times faster than jobs. The proportion of Americans in the workforce is now the lowest it has been in more than forty years.[3] Competition for jobs is now global, and positions are harder to find.

Shorter job tenure and rapid turnover have also become the norm. A Bureau of Labor Statistics study tracking ten thousand individuals over more than thirty-five years shows that people held an average of eleven jobs—a number that may well be on the rise for younger employees.[4]

At the same time, another trend has risen among US workers: a longing for more job satisfaction. A full 51 percent of US workers describe themselves as "not engaged" at work, and 17.5

percent say they're "actively disengaged."[5] Clearly they're looking for more, both in terms of money—by some measures, wages have been stagnant literally since the 1970s—and personal fulfillment, including a quality of life that many believe comes with independent work.[6]

In a survey of self-employed people, the majority cited flexibility as the chief benefit of their choice, and 50 percent said they wouldn't go back to working a traditional job, no matter how much it paid.[7] No surprise, then, that 34 percent of US workers are currently freelancers, and a study by Intuit asserts that by 2020, that number will rise to 40 percent.[8]

Clearly, if we're not entrepreneurs already, we all need to start thinking that way. Even if you're perfectly happy with your day job now, consider entrepreneurship as an insurance policy for your career, just as Bozi Dar did. Maybe you've wanted to start a food blog in your off-hours, or to offer personal or professional coaching to friends and acquaintances on the side. Perhaps you'd like to take on speaking gigs or organize a conference or event for like-minded people. Whatever form it takes, creating such "side streams" of income enables you to take more control of your career, your finances, and your life.

Today, I actually earn my living in seven entirely different ways: writing books, speaking, teaching business school, consulting, executive coaching, online courses, and—since that a-ha moment from my friend John Corcoran—affiliate income through my email list. If one of those avenues goes away, I have enough diversification that I don't have to worry. That's a far cry from my position at age twenty-two, when I woke up the day after my layoff wondering how I'd pay my bills.

I'm not the only one advocating the importance of multiple revenue streams. Alexandra Levit, author of six books, including *They Don't Teach Corporate in College*, told me in an interview,

"I'm all about diversification in every area of my life. I've seen too many times where things that you think were going to be huge don't work out, and that can be really scary . . . So I try to mitigate risk whenever I can. I hedge my bets, so if this doesn't work out, I've got three other things that probably will. If something falls through—and I've had that happen dozens of times, things that just completely imploded—I'm still doing OK."

Jenny Blake, a career and business strategist who is the author of *Pivot: The Only Move That Matters Is Your Next One*, views her income streams as serving distinct purposes. In the early days of her career, she relied on one-on-one coaching to provide steady revenue—what she called her "bridge income"—while she built up her professional speaking business. Speaking was her true passion, but invitations were unpredictable and sporadic, so she felt it would be dangerous to rely on them exclusively. But balanced with her coaching, "they evened each other out," she says, and created a steadier income stream.

All of which is to say, enjoying the freedom and independence that comes with developing a portfolio career doesn't mean giving up income. As Levit, Blake, and countless others demonstrate, creating a portfolio career enables you to dramatically increase your earnings. This book will show you how.

You Don't Have to Trade Income for Freedom

It seems like poetic justice: the same internet technology that has caused so many workforce displacements (the decimation of newspapers, to name just one) also offers us more opportunities than ever to fulfill our unique visions as entrepreneurs. Today you can scale your efforts, skills, and expertise in unprecedented ways that give you choice in how you want to live your life.

If you'd like to live on a beach, you can now work in ways that are entirely location-independent. If you want to build a powerful platform and become internationally recognized, technology has made that goal more achievable than ever. If you'd like to spend more time with your kids, many successful entrepreneurs have leveraged the internet to do just that. Best of all, doing these things doesn't necessarily mean giving up income to gain the independence of an entrepreneurial existence.

These days, however, we need more than the magic of technology to experience the full economic potential of entrepreneurship. We need to think creatively about different ways to monetize our ideas or, as internet theorist David "Doc" Searls has noted, to shift from making money *with* something (such as when I was paid as a journalist to write articles) to making money *because of* something (when I began to write articles in order to attract speaking gigs—at ultimately far better pay than what I earned as a journalist).[9]

John Lee Dumas, a US Army veteran who served in Iraq, demonstrated just such creative thinking when he launched his business. Dumas hadn't had much luck with traditional jobs after leaving the service. He tried working in corporate finance, then at a tech startup, and finally in real estate. None of it stuck. But in the interim, he'd become a passionate podcast listener and decided to create his own. He called it *Entrepreneur on Fire*, and made one crucial change to the typical formula. Most podcasts aired weekly, or sometimes even less frequently. But, Dumas wondered, what if you could create something valuable for listeners every single day?

Deploying a small team of virtual assistants who helped with production, Dumas spent one day a week taping seven back-to-back interviews, creating that week's material. The frequency created momentum and juiced download numbers, which in turn drew advertiser interest and increased revenue. Just a year after he launched, he won a "Best of iTunes" award, further cementing his reputation.

What's more, each month he publishes a public income report that tracks how much and where his revenue comes from. Through a mix of sources, including advertising, online courses, and membership in the Podcasters' Paradise online community he's founded, he brings in monthly earnings that would please most professionals, if that were their yearly salary. Since December 2013, he's grossed at least six figures per month, sometimes approaching $600,000 in a thirty-day period.

We could dismiss Dumas as an anomaly. But as I began to research the phenomenon of location-independent online entrepreneurs, I realized he's not alone. Bjork and Lindsay Ostrom, a Minnesota couple who started the *Pinch of Yum* food blog, regularly bring in well over $50,000 per month through advertising, sponsored posts, ebook sales, and more.

To be clear, none of this comes easy. I've spent more than a decade building my business; it's similar for most of the entrepreneurs I profile in this book. What gives marketing a bad name is the get-rich-quackery that promises immediate results.

Instead, to diversify and maximize your income, first think broadly about how to provide value to others. Next, choose a few different revenue streams to focus on. You certainly don't need to pursue every possible strategy; doing so would just pull you in too many directions. But developing at least a few creative methods can mean the difference between surviving and thriving in your business. What matters most is focus and execution.

Making Money in the Internet Era: A Road Map

When it comes to building a successful business, there's plenty of smoke and mirrors out there—entrepreneurs puffing their chests and sharing only their success stories. But as I dove into researching how to expand and diversify my own business, I wanted the unvarnished truth.

I decided to use my journalistic training to go behind the scenes with this new breed of self-directed professionals to see what really works and how we all can apply winning strategies to our own lives. Along the way, I also share my own experiences of building a multiple six-figure consulting and speaking business and learning, from the ground up, how to tap into the monetizing potential of the internet. I'll trace the highlights, from the glorious first check I received for $365 in commissions (for sending one email!) to the frustrating failure of my first online course and subsequent redemption as I learned the ropes.

Throughout the book, we'll learn together what works, what doesn't, and how to foster a thriving, diversified business model in smart, ethical, and maximally efficient ways. It turns out that what makes monetization sustainable is creating a solid foundation over time through a three-step process: building your brand; monetizing your expertise; and extending your reach and impact online.

With this introductory chapter, we've already begun part one of the book, "Build Your Brand." Chapter 2 continues the theme, delving into the *why and how* of establishing your brand—a road map for developing a trusted reputation so that, even in a crowded marketplace, others will seek you out. Once you've gained some credentials, part two (chapters 3–8) will show you how to "Monetize Your Expertise"—in other words, mastering your craft by providing traditional, in-person service offerings such as consulting.

Part three, "Extend Your Reach and Impact Online" (chapters 9–11), brings together your hard-won combination of brand and expertise to guide you through using the power of the internet and other means to scale your impact. Finally, the book's concluding chapter (chapter 12) addresses things to consider as your entrepreneurial career grows, such as adding assistants or additional employees, in order to maximize your quality of life and develop the type of business that suits your aspirations and lifestyle.

Additionally, you'll see short "Try This" sections throughout the book, which prompt you to consider how the concepts I cover apply to your own life and business. I've created a free resource—an *Entrepreneurial You* self-assessment workbook—that you can download and follow along with as you progress through the book.

Most important, you'll also see that there's no one "right" path to monetization for professionals to follow. Some might feel attracted to certain strategies, like coaching or blogging; others may select something else from the smorgasbord, like keynote speaking or creating online membership communities. What's essential is understanding that it's riskier *not* to diversify, and that selecting and developing a few specific strategies will allow

Self-Assessment

To access the *Entrepreneurial You* self-assessment, go to dorieclark.com/entrepreneur.

you to connect with new audiences, reach people in different ways, and capture value through multiple channels.

With the right strategy, you can thrive in the new portfolio-career economy. It's possible to live the life you want, become truly respected in your field, and earn life-changing income in the process. The next chapter will help you begin, by learning a key element of crafting your brand: building trust with your target market or audience.

CHAPTER 2

First, Become a Trusted Source

In the depths of the Great Recession in 2008, Pat Flynn had just been laid off from his job at an architecture firm. On a whim, he'd started selling an ebook a few months earlier about how to pass the Leadership in Energy and Environmental Design (LEED) exam that certifies knowledge of eco-friendly building practices. The ebook had done surprisingly well. Suddenly out of a job, and with his wedding just months away, he wondered, *could I make a living online?*

But as he started researching internet marketing, he told me, "I felt kind of disgusted by being on the other end of their emails. I felt like everybody was holding back some information; they wanted me to pay money to get the rest of it." He purchased some of their courses, just to see what he might be missing. But it was a disappointment. "It was the 'You can click this button and get rich, or make $1,000 a week'; all this stuff that I knew from my own experience totally wasn't true," Flynn said.

Unlike the hucksters he initially encountered, Flynn vowed to share everything he knew with his readers, without holding back the essential parts for paying customers. Today, he is a successful blogger and podcaster who earns well over $100,000 per month (he cracked $250,000 in March 2017 alone). Positing himself as the "crash-test dummy of internet marketing," Flynn reveals in detail both his hits and misses. He pioneered the now-popular concept of publishing monthly income reports detailing his revenue and expenses, because "in order for me to really show people that this stuff actually worked, I needed to show people how much money I was making."

That level of transparency has created a huge level of trust with his audience. When he surveyed his audience after the launch of his first product—the LEED study guide, which bundled together in an easy-to-read form the material he was already sharing for free online—he discovered that "about 25 percent of the people who responded back told me they had already taken and passed the exam, but [buying the guide] was the first opportunity for them to pay me back for that information."

As Flynn discovered from his own initial online purchases, slick salespeople who overpromise may be able to wring out an initial sale by dropping teasers about the "special, secret techniques" they'll reveal—for a price. But their tactics quickly alienate customers, who will never return. At the other end of the spectrum are the talented, hard-working professionals who genuinely have a lot to offer their clients, but whose quiet message is often drowned out by the cacophony of voices competing for attention.

Somehow, in order to build a sustainable and lucrative business, like Flynn we need to carve out a path between these two extremes—aggressive salespeople without substance, and substantive professionals who can't sell. We have to find a way to build trust with the people in our audience and make them want to do business with us. (If you're still figuring out what knowledge or skills you want to share with the world, check out the sidebar "Assessing Your Areas of Expertise" at the end of this chapter.)

Now we're going to dive into some key ways to cultivate a strong relationship with your audience: create valuable online content; write a book; network and build social proof; maintain a connection with your audience; and build your email list.

Create Valuable Online Content

First, we can create valuable content that displays our expertise and allows people to see for themselves that we're knowledgeable. Flynn wrote and recorded podcasts on his own site, *Smart Passive Income*, but you can also accelerate the trust-building process by creating content for sites that people already know and respect.

That's the route I took. In 2010, drawing on the experience I'd gained during my short tenure in journalism, politics, and later running a small bicycling-advocacy nonprofit, I started blogging about marketing and branding for the *Huffington Post* and the *Harvard Business Review*. The affiliations were a helpful boost to my résumé. Much like an Ivy League degree, my blog contributions signaled readers to take me more seriously, because I had already been vetted and approved by institutions they recognized. In other words, in a busy world, they provided a shortcut and saved people from the hassle of having to independently evaluate my merits. Over time, as you contribute more frequently—I've now written more than 120 pieces for the

Harvard Business Review alone—people begin to associate you with those outlets, and your brand connection is solidified.

Starting to write for prominent outlets in your industry may seem like a stretch, but in a 24/7 media cycle, those sites are always searching for high-quality content. Sure, I had to endure repeated brush-offs from magazine and blog editors before breaking in at HBR, but persistence and effort matter.

Then, in late 2011, I decided that I wanted to write more frequently and find an additional business outlet where I could contribute. I took two full workdays to create a list of two dozen business publications—including the websites for magazines, regional and national newspapers, and TV networks—and plugged them into a spreadsheet. For each, I identified whether they had a blog on their site, whether that blog used outside contributors (if only in-house staffers wrote for it, it wasn't a viable target), and the name and email address of the web editor. Sometimes I had to dig to find the correct person in charge, but through Google and LinkedIn searches, and scouring each website's site map and submission guidelines, I could usually find it.

I sent short email inquiries to each editor, briefly explaining who I was, why I was interested in contributing to their publication, what I could write about, and links to past articles so they could evaluate my writing style. Although I didn't specify in my emails that I was glad to write for free, I assumed my initial engagements would be structured that way (and it would have been a happy surprise if they weren't). You should too. Don't count on payment until you've started to establish yourself a bit. Of the two dozen inquiries, only three got back to me—not an encouraging hit rate for a former professional journalist, but that's how we roll in the new economy.

Of the three, two correspondences quickly fizzled; I sent further information, or tried to schedule a phone call, but they stopped writing back. But it turned out that one person I had hunted down, the managing editor at *Forbes*, was actively looking for new contributors. We scheduled a call within days, and less than two weeks later, my first piece appeared on the site. I ended up writing for *Forbes* for three and a half years, pumping out more than 250 articles. By writing for *Forbes* frequently— five to ten times per month—I earned a small amount of money as a paid contributor. But that was a side benefit; the real value was in dramatically increasing my name recognition and exposure to corporate audiences.

Try This:

As you think about creating your own content, ask yourself:

- What media outlets do your target audience members regularly read, watch, or listen to?

- Which of these accept pieces from outside contributors?

- Can you create a list of three to five ideas, targeted to their style and focus area, to pitch them?

- Who do you know who contributes to these outlets? Are they willing to introduce you?

- In the next week, write a short pitch email to at least three outlets and offer your services.

Write a Book

Writing a book can also be a major brand enhancer. It's no longer *mandatory* these days, the way it was in the era of gatekeepers;

John Lee Dumas, for instance, built a large and lucrative following through podcasting alone.

If you do enjoy writing, however, it's still one of the most effective tools for demonstrating your expertise, engaging new audiences, and building your credibility. That's valuable at any stage in your career. But it's especially important early on, when others may doubt your expertise. Dan Schawbel, a consultant and entrepreneur, started writing his first book, *Me 2.0*, when he was twenty-three and published it two years later. "Having a book says, 'Maybe I'm not like the other twenty-two- or twenty-three-year-olds,' and maybe you'll give me a little bit more of a chance," he told me.

These days, self-publishing has lost its previous stigma and is a desirable choice for many authors (including Flynn). Even ebooks, if they're well written, can become a powerful marketing tool. But at least for now, there's still nothing like a traditionally published book to cement your reputation.

For years, I spoke frequently at local events—for free—to promote my consulting business. The talks were well received, but the audiences were small and certainly no one offered to pay me. But all that changed once I published my first book, *Reinventing You*, in 2013. All of a sudden, event organizers looked at me differently; I was now an expert worthy of being sought out, rather than a run-of-the-mill consultant trawling for business.

I had wanted to publish a book for years, and had tried, but my previous proposals were rejected because I didn't yet have a large enough "platform" (i.e., I wasn't sufficiently well known). To remedy the situation, I started blogging, and in the process, I discovered something valuable: content creation wasn't just a means of building my brand. It was also a form of market research that revealed what audiences were most interested in.

A post I wrote for *Harvard Business Review*, "How to Reinvent Your Personal Brand," wasn't intended to be my statement to the world. I didn't think of it as being different from, or more special than, dozens of other posts I had done previously for my own blog or other publications. But it caught on, and HBR asked if I'd be willing to consider expanding it to a 2,500-word piece. When it came out, three different literary agents approached me, and that's when I realized that I'd inadvertently hit a nerve.

A book on professional reinvention turned out to be a much better topic than the ones I had dreamed up and pitched previously—a guide for millennials in the workplace, and a book about how business executives could learn communication techniques using case studies from the world of politics. But I had no way of knowing that, or testing those assumptions, until I wrote a post and saw the audience reaction firsthand.

Try This:

If you're thinking of writing a book, consider these key questions and thoughts:

- Determine if you'd like to self-publish or commercially publish your book. Self-publishing is good if you're writing for a niche audience ("social media marketing for real estate agents"), if you want to publish quickly (traditional publishing takes at least one to two years), and if you want a greater share of both control and revenues. Traditional publishing is good if you're seeking credibility (there is perceived value in being chosen and vetted by a major publishing house), and you'd like to focus on writing and promotion (the publisher will handle design, distribution, foreign rights, etc.).

- Which of your blog posts, podcasts, or videos have been particularly popular? That may reveal emerging trends or book topics that your audience would respond to.

- Once you've identified a possible topic, create a list of competitive works. Even if you plan to self-publish (and therefore don't need to create a book proposal), it's still useful to survey the field and determine who else is operating in your field. What angle did they take? How will yours be different or unique?

- If you're planning to approach traditional publishers, read the acknowledgments section of the competing works. Almost always, authors thank their agents there (and agents are necessary if you want to sell to a large commercial publisher). Doing this will give you a short list of agents who have successfully sold books very much like yours, and you can loop back and approach them once your proposal is finished.

- Create a back-of-the-envelope outline for your book. This doesn't have to be a final product; it's just an exercise to determine whether you have enough content or ideas to fill a book. For starters, imagine that you're writing a ten-chapter book. What would you want to cover in each chapter? Try to write at least a one-paragraph description for each. If you can't come up with enough material, you may need to think it through more or create a short ebook. If you have way too much material, you may have chosen a topic that's too broad ("The History of Western Civilization") and you might consider narrowing your focus.

- Start to develop your book marketing plan. How will you get copies into the hands of your readers? Are there special resources you can tap (a client's company would be willing to buy five hundred copies, or you speak frequently and could waive your speaking fee in exchange for a bulk book purchase)? What media outlets are most important to reach? Start making a list of the blogs or magazines where you'd like to be featured, the podcasts you'd like to appear on, and so on. Start monitoring them to see if they profile books similar to yours (which implies they might be open to a pitch when your book is ready) or if they have written about colleagues you know (in which case, you can ask those colleagues for an introduction).

- Now, you're ready to start creating your book proposal (if you're planning to commercially publish) or dive into writing the first chapter (if you'll be self-publishing). Good luck!

Network and Build Social Proof

In psychology, there's a concept known as "social proof"—the well-established fact that others judge you by your affiliations. If you write for the *Harvard Business Review* or *Forbes*, people are more likely to view you as competent or authoritative because their impression of those brands transfers to you. The same holds true for the individuals you associate with, and networking—surrounding yourself with people you respect, and whose audiences overlap with yours—can be a valuable strategy in building a trusted reputation.

Selena Soo, a New York City-based entrepreneur, discovered that truth soon after launching her business as a publicity strategist in 2012. She realized that guest posting on the blogs of established industry players, or appearing on their podcasts, led to significant visibility and drove sign-ups to her email list at a far greater rate than paid advertising. Soo says that people may respond to a Facebook ad, but there's a degree of skepticism if you're an unknown quantity. But it's different if you've been endorsed by someone they trust. it. "[I]f you're on a podcast and you've got someone like John Lee Dumas from *Entrepreneur on Fire* saying, 'Hey guys, you've got to check this person out. She's amazing'—it's just totally different."

She added, "I find that people that come through those online publicity sources are twice as responsive [as leads generated through paid advertising] and they stay on your list. They're less likely to unsubscribe, and they're more likely to buy." It makes sense: the level of initial trust is higher, because you've been endorsed by respected sources.

That strategy also worked for Derek Halpern. In 2006, he launched a celebrity gossip site, where he quickly grew a following, attracting nearly 40 million annual site visitors by the following year and earning as much as $20,000 per month. But he soon grew tired of peddling hyped-up celebrity tidbits. He eventually shut down the site, and in March 2011, he launched something of far greater personal interest: Social Triggers, a website devoted to marketing and psychology. He was a complete unknown, however, in both marketing and psychology, so he had to find a way to be taken seriously.

Networking and social proof go hand in hand with another important principle—*provide value to others first*—that Halpern took to heart. He drew upon the online marketing experience he'd accrued in running his gossip site and reached out to prominent business bloggers such as Pat Flynn and Chris Brogan, who were already big names in the niche he now sought to inhabit.

"I approached people who ran blogs that had the audience I wanted to reach, and said, 'Hey, you're losing out on some conversions [of site visitors into subscribers]. I think I can help.'" Halpern then asked for a fifteen-minute video call in which he would offer the bloggers some free website-marketing advice. "I told them to record the video. If my advice worked for them, I asked them to post the video." By essentially offering free consulting, Halpern got the chance to get his message out to the bloggers' large audiences.

The videos were a hit, both with the bloggers and their audiences. "If you watch every video," he told me, "you'll notice I had some good ideas for them—and that I said the same thing in almost every one. Most people get a good idea, and they promote it once and never talk about it again. I got a good idea and talked about it in twenty videos." Halpern was immediately branded as an expert, because he was not only shown associating with prominent figures, but they were listening to him and deferring to his recommendations. Within three months, he had garnered more than ten thousand email subscribers, who were driven to his site almost exclusively by the videos. "I'm still reaping the benefits from those videos," he said. "I still get traffic."

Try This:

In order to build social proof and enhance your reputation, ask yourself the following questions:

- What forms of social proof can you leverage (such as affiliations with prominent companies, educational institutions, membership organizations, media outlets, or individuals)?

- Who are the influencers that it would make the biggest difference for you to connect with?

- What skills or resources can you offer to help more experienced people in your field?

Maintain a Connection with Your Audience

Once you've introduced yourself to an audience and built an initial connection with them, you need to keep in touch and deepen their level of trust in you. In the world of politics, there's a saying that voters have to hear your name seven times before they'll remember it, and the same is true in business: repeat exposure is essential.

Despite the hype around social media—and the genuine opportunity it represents for expanding your audience and occasionally allowing your ideas to go viral—it's actually a serious mistake to rely on social media as the primary means of communicating with your audience. Facebook's 2013 decision to rejigger the algorithms that determined which posts appeared in your newsfeed proved massively disruptive to brands that had spent huge amounts of time and money building up their "likes" in order to reach their fan base.

Business Insider's headline said it all: "Facebook Slightly Tweaked How the Site Works—And It Screwed an Entire Profession."[1] That profession, of course, was social media marketers, who suddenly realized the folly of allowing their relationship with customers to be mediated by private companies that are beholden to venture capitalists or shareholders. It's not just Facebook; online marketing expert Danny Sullivan studied engagement on his Twitter account—which, at the time, had nearly four hundred thousand followers—and discovered that, on average, only 1.3 percent to 2.6 percent of his followers saw any given tweet.[2]

If we can't even count on reaching our own followers on social media, what *does* work? Across the nearly fifty experts and thought leaders I interviewed for this book, there was an overwhelming consensus: old-fashioned email.

When people are busy, they may take a "social media sabbatical" for a few days. But for most professionals, their email inbox is sacred: it's where they receive their most important messages. Even for top leaders, handling email is one of the last things they typically delegate to assistants; many executives refer to it as their "control panel" that enables them to monitor the pulse of their business.

But the overwhelming effect of too much email is real: a 2015 study showed the average email user sends or receives a whopping 122 messages per day.[3] So if you've been proactively invited into someone's inbox, that's the surest sign of trust and an indication that they're likely to take the time to read what you've sent. (On the other hand, don't be tempted to add people to your email list without their permission. It's not only bad form; you might also be violating anti-spam laws.)

Try This:

As you consider how to deepen your connection to your audience, keep the following in mind:

- Take stock of your email list. Do you have one? If so, did everyone on it proactively opt in and ask to be added? If yes, great. If not, remove them. It's fine to send a onetime email to all your contacts to ask if they'd like to join your mailing list, but you should make them click to proactively opt in to receive further mailings; you can let everyone else know it will be the only mailing you send.

- Start to reallocate your time. How much time per week do you spend on social media for your business? An hour? Two hours? Five hours? Make a decision to reprioritize. Take at least 30 percent of that time and shift it toward building your email list. (We'll discuss the exact mechanics in more depth later.) The return on investment will be incalculable.

Build Your Email List

I learned my lesson about email list building during the launch of my first book, *Reinventing You*. In the past, I had taken a lackadaisical attitude toward growing my list. Sure, I took people's business cards and added them when they asked, and I sometimes put a link at the end of articles I wrote, encouraging people to "sign up for my e-newsletter." But more often, I drove them to my Twitter account or a link to buy my book online. I was content to "raise awareness," and that was a crucial error, because when it came time to notify my readers that my first book was coming out, I wasn't sure where or how to reach them.

Think about it: How many times do you read a review of an interesting book in the newspaper or hear about it on the radio, and then actually remember to go buy it? Usually, those thoughts are fleeting: *oh, that sounds interesting!* But unless you soon find yourself wandering in a bookstore with that exact title in front of you, it's likely that you'll forget.

By the time I launched my second book, *Stand Out*, in 2015, I was determined to do better. I had 9,500 subscribers on my email list before the launch—not bad, but certainly not as many as it could have been if I'd applied more effort. First of all, I realized that I needed a good inducement for people to subscribe. "Join my email list" is rarely convincing; people often receive dozens of such solicitations, and most are banal, overly self-promotional, or both. Why would a sensible person sign up for one more? Instead, I needed to lure my audience with something they'd consider interesting and valuable.

I convinced my publisher to loan me one of its graphic designers for an hour or two in order to create a handsome, forty-two-page PDF workbook based on my book. It literally only took about a half hour of my time to create; I simply assembled the questions at the back of each chapter in the book and put them into one document, with room for readers to write their own answers. It was the perfect sort of giveaway: easy to create, but extremely useful for recipients. (I've created a similar self-assessment for this book. See the download information in the sidebar "Assessments.")

During my launch and in the months afterward, I wrote dozens of guest posts for various blogs, always promoting the workbook at the end of the piece in my bio. I also did more than 160 podcast interviews and made a point of driving listeners to the page where they, too, could enter their email address to download the workbook and join my list.

Assessments

You can download a free copy of the *Stand Out* self-assessment workbook—which enabled me to grow my email list by 150 percent in less than a year—by visiting dorieclark.com/join. To access the *Entrepreneurial You* self-assessment, go to dorieclark.com/entrepreneur.

That strategy—providing something of real value to readers—helped me more than double my list; my subscriber count rose from 9,500 in February 2015 to more than 25,000 by the end of that year. That represents a massive increase in the number of people who know my name and my work, and whom I can easily reach with messages and updates.

Free workbooks are one example of a desirable giveaway; others might include links to videos, such as webinars or an instructional series; tip sheets; a "mini-course" made up of emails teaching you how to do something over a period of a few days or weeks; "swipe files" with sample text or graphics to help you solve a particular problem, such as how to reach out to influencers or how to craft great sales copy; or more in-depth articles or ebooks relating to the original post they read.

Try This:

As you think about how to increase your opt-ins, it's worth asking:

- What knowledge or information do you have that people ask you about frequently (anything from how to become a better table tennis player to how to negotiate a better salary)?

- How could you package this into a desirable "lead magnet" and what form would it take (workbook, video series, tip sheets, resource guide, swipe files, etc.)?

- How will you advertise your lead magnet (appear on podcasts, write a detailed article, create Facebook ads, etc.)?

Creating a lead magnet to grow your email list is a great start, but how can you ensure people find it in the first place? In addition to mentioning my free workbook during the podcast interviews I appeared on, I also included a link to it in the bio that appeared at the end of articles and blogs that I wrote.

That strategy paid off for me, but I'm a rookie compared with Chris Winfield, who used one compelling blog post to grow his email list by fifteen thousand subscribers. His post "How to Work 40 Hours in 16.7," which appeared on the website *Medium* (and was republished elsewhere), went massively viral. For some entrepreneurs, that might have been the end of it. But Winfield made sure to include a so-called "content upgrade" at the end of his lengthy post—a lead magnet promising even more information for those who were curious.

"Want to go further?" he asked in the post. "Ready to save 23.3 hours each week and get MORE accomplished? Of course you are . . . and I want to make it as easy as possible for you." He then added a clickable image linked to his free thirty-two-page guide that explained his system in detail and included worksheets, tools, and resources. His clear promise, aimed squarely at people who were already interested in the topic and had read to the end of his two-thousand-word article, resulted in an astonishing fifteen thousand subscribers from just that one post.

Winfield isn't the only one who has used blogging as a strategy to gain new email subscribers. Perhaps the most impressive example of list building is James Clear, a blogger who writes about the habits that can improve physical and mental performance. He started blogging in late 2012 and made a commitment to post two articles a week. Within two years, he'd reached a hundred thousand subscribers; by April 2017, he had more than four hundred thousand.

Clear's list-building success hinges on four strategies: consistency, focus, great headlines, and syndication.

Consistency

For Clear, there's only one explanation for why his readership has skyrocketed so dramatically: his consistency. When he launched his site, Clear recalls, there was a health blogger he admired: "He was writing really great science-based pieces that people really liked. His audience was five times the size of mine when I was getting started. Today, my audience is twenty times the size of his, and you can't say that it's because of quality, because he's producing very high-quality stuff. The only difference is that I decided to write every Monday and every Thursday starting on November 12, 2012, while he has just written intermittently."

His consistent pace gives him two advantages. First, he says, "every piece of content that you produce is a chance to rank in Google and drive search engine traffic, or for people to share it on social media, or for someone to email an article to their friends." More volume means more exposure. But second, he says, writing at least eight articles per month ensures that some of them will strike a strong chord with readers. "Every marketing strategy is easier with good content," he says. "We often think, 'I just need a better strategy, or I just need a better tactic,' when really what you need is better work." His frequency gave him the opportunity to produce more great ideas.[*]

Focus

You don't want to paralyze readers with too many choices when they visit your website and read your blog. "I want there to be one clear call to action on each page," Clear told me. "I don't

---

[*]Consistency is powerful, but hard even for superstars to keep up. In order to spend more time writing his first book, Clear made a strategic decision to dial back his blog output after three years.

want to confuse people by having them 'Click here to buy my book, click here to sign up for my email list, follow me on Twitter and Facebook, and read this article.' That's five things that they should do. When they have five things to do, they'll probably do nothing because they don't know what the most important thing is." Instead, Clear's site draws attention to only one thing: signing up to receive a free ebook on transforming your habits, which will also opt you into his email list. He includes no sidebars or anything else that will distract viewers from the main focus: signing up for his list.

Great Headlines

When it comes to building your email list, it's impossible to overstate the importance of blog post headlines, which attract readers in the first place. As Winfield discovered, it's worth spending a disproportionate amount of time identifying a compelling title.

Winfield struggled mightily to find a simple title for his elaborately detailed article on productivity. The article promoted the Pomodoro Technique, a strategy in which you focus intently on a given task for twenty-five minutes, then take a five-minute break to recharge, and repeat the process one to four more times before taking a fifteen-minute break. (The name comes from the tomato-shaped timer used by the technique's originator, Francesco Cirillo.)

Winfield originally thought "The 40 Pomodoro Work Week" would be a great title for the post, because it evoked Tim Ferriss's popular productivity book, *The 4-Hour Workweek*. But then he realized, "That's me thinking in a bubble. Most people have no idea what the Pomodoro Technique is." He continued to brainstorm.

Fundamentally, the post's promise is about "how to work twice as much in half the time"—a compelling promise, but one that people may have heard before (and been skeptical of). He realized that a precise, numerical specificity could set the post apart, and his final title, "How to Work 40 Hours in 16.7," became a runaway hit.

Syndication

Clear always posts his articles on his own site first. But he doesn't stop there. He currently has syndication agreements with sites including *Entrepreneur, Lifehacker, Business Insider,* and *Forbes*; if they think their audience would be interested in the article, they're allowed to repost it. His bio at the bottom drives readers back to his home page and encourages them to sign up for his newsletter. It might sound impossible for you to lure the attention of top-ranked publications, and, indeed, it's not something to worry about at first.

But early on, you can repost your articles on sites like LinkedIn and *Medium*, which are open to anyone. As you progress, you may develop connections with other bloggers, who would welcome the chance to share your material with their readers. And over time, as you gain more readers and experience, you're likely to find that editors from increasingly prominent outlets seek you out. Indeed, I started writing for *Entrepreneur* when an editor there, who had been following my writing for other publications, messaged me on Twitter to see if I'd consider writing for them. This can help turbocharge your exposure and list growth after you gain more experience.

Building your email list, providing your readers with compelling content, surrounding yourself with respected peers and colleagues—all of these are essential strategies in building trust and establishing your brand. Of course, the eventual goal is to find ways to convert your audience into paying customers, so that your business can become sustainable. But that transition—from offering your content for free to charging actual money—can be fraught. If your business is going to succeed over the long term, however, you need to find ways to monetize that feel authentic to you and offer real value to your customers. I'll discuss that in the next chapter.

Try This:

If you plan to grow your email list through content marketing, ask yourself:

- Have you set a consistent content-creation schedule for yourself? Whether you're blogging or creating videos or podcasts (techniques we'll talk about later in the book), having a regular schedule, such as "weekly" or "Tuesdays and Thursdays," helps your readers know what to expect.

- Audit your website and bio. Do you have multiple calls to action ("subscribe to my YouTube channel" and "follow me on Twitter" and "connect on LinkedIn")? Purge these and focus your message on what's most important: getting people to sign up for your email list.

- Analyze the headlines of the content you create. Which past titles have gotten the biggest readership? What patterns do you see? Are there certain words or phrases people seem attracted to? Do your readers like long or short titles? Do they respond well to "list" posts ("4 Ways to Improve Your Marketing Today")? Take note and adapt.

Assessing Your Areas of Expertise

For some professionals, it's obvious what skills or knowledge they'd want to share in an entrepreneurial venture. But for others, it can be a bit murkier. You may have a variety of interests or perhaps you're a generalist. How do you know what to focus on? And what are the first steps you should take once you think you've found it? Here are some pointers from Bozi Dar, the life sciences marketing executive who runs an online business on the side.

Don't fall in love with your idea. Dar's first product was an app that helped people change their mood by looking at their personal photos paired with music. It was a cool idea, but he's convinced the reason it failed is that "I started my app not really testing whether there is a problem [that customers wanted solved], not testing what is my audience, not testing whether anyone was even searching for a solution. I just fell in love with my idea, starting putting money and time into it, and it never worked." Don't just come up with a clever notion; make sure people actually want it first.

Understand what you're uniquely qualified to share. On the other hand, Dar's successful online career course arose from the questions others kept asking him. "I was getting promotion after promotion," he recalls. His friends and colleagues noticed, and "I found myself being invited for these coffee/ mentoring sessions nonstop." He realized others found his perspective valuable, and perhaps an audience might pay for it.

Don't rush to quit your job. Some people get so excited about their new entrepreneurial venture that they want to go all in immediately and quit their day job. Dar disagrees. He recommends staying in your job for at least a year, if not more. "I would rather stay in the company and start testing your hypothesis [about your business model]," he says. "What's the problem? Are people searching for the solution? Who is the customer? . . . I'd try to get answers to those questions before I left the job, and the ultimate test [of the idea's viability] would be that someone opens their wallet to pay for what I'm offering."

Build your competencies. A lot of people who are employed by companies, even if they're very talented, may not be fully ready for entrepreneurship in the beginning. That's why Dar suggests making a concerted effort—while you're still in your job—to build out your entrepreneurial skill set. That was my strategy, as well. I decided to launch my own business in 2005, but stayed in my job for an additional year, while taking professional development classes—that my employer paid for—on topics I knew I'd need to learn, such as financial management, design, and business strategy. Dar recommends that you use this period to learn "foundational skills," such as sales, oral presentation, persuasion, copywriting, and more. "Buying courses, joining a mastermind, and having a business coach will all help," he says.

Indeed, Marie Forleo—a life coach who has been praised by Oprah Winfrey and now runs an eight-figure business—recounts her early days when she invested heavily in skills building.[a] "I didn't want to be desperate for clients," she said, "so I bartended and did other odd jobs to bring in enough money to maintain my NYC lifestyle and invest in my own business and marketing education."[b]

Focus on one channel at a time. Finally, when you're ready to launch, you can easily get overwhelmed with all the things you *could* be doing. Instead, Dar suggests mastering one channel at a time, so you get really good at it, and you can build from there. In his case, he has one course (the Career Acceleration Formula); he markets it via one channel (webinars); and he identifies those webinar opportunities through one mechanism (affiliate partnerships). That focus "is the only way that you can build a solid base and then conquer other traffic channels or other products," he says. Facebook ads or search engine marketing might be appealing possibilities, but for now, they're too much. It's better to excel in one area and then bridge from there.

[a] Nathan Chan, "FPO33: Marie Forleo Reveals How to Build an 8 Figure Business with Heart," *Foundr*, March 5, 2015, https://foundrmag.com/fp033-marie-forleo-reveals-how-to-build-an-8-figure-business-with-heart/.

[b] Marie Forleo, "The Rich, Happy & Hot Entrepreneur Blueprint," https://www.tonyrobbins.com/pdfs/Marie%20Forleo%20MM%20Workbook.pdf.

PART TWO

Monetize Your Expertise

CHAPTER 3

The Courage to Monetize

Building up the courage to monetize can be a challenge. What if no one wants your product? Or if people complain that you're overpriced? Or call you a sellout for charging at all? All of that can, and likely will, happen. But you can't help others with your insightful advice or great product or service if you can't keep yourself in business. Charging what you're worth is key to creating the long-term impact you desire.

In this chapter we'll look at how to begin monetizing your business. It starts with gaining confidence about the value you bring to the table; focusing on the right metrics; overcoming some common types of resistance; and striking the right balance regarding things like timing.

Understand the Value You Offer

The first step is to get clear on the value you bring to others. Once you do that, you'll feel more comfortable charging appropriate—even premium—prices.

Shortly after I launched my consulting business in 2006, I landed a meeting with a potential client. I spent an hour asking her incisive questions about her organization and talked about possible solutions I could offer. I'd nearly sealed the deal, when she asked a rather obvious question: What do you charge?

I was blindsided.

I suppose I'd been hoping to avoid the question, or have her make the first offer, or intone something about paying their "standard rate for consultants," whatever that might be. Somehow, I'd managed to avoid even *thinking* about my rates; I had no idea what to say.

I thought fast. "$60 an hour," I mumbled. That was just a bit less than what my acupuncturist charged; I figured if I didn't mind paying it, she wouldn't either. But when she said yes—too quickly—I realized I'd made a crucial mistake. I'd left money on the table.

Over the next few years, I stumbled along, accepting laughably small assignments for miniscule pay—writing a speech for $500, or doing copywriting for a few flyers for $250. I made up for it in volume; in my first few years of business, I worked with more than eighty clients and still managed to bring in a six-figure salary, despite my absurdly low rates. But the pace was relentless.

Over time, I began to raise my rates—and my standards—just a bit. I had a track record, so I no longer bothered to accept $500 engagements. But I still did plenty of $2,500 and $5,000 consulting assignments that took weeks or months of my time.

In the early days of your business, you're willing to do almost anything to gain experience and build a list of clients who could provide referrals and testimonials. You'll probably lose those early, low-paying clients when you move upmarket and increase your rates over time, which can be a daunting prospect.

But it's necessary in order to break the pattern of being so busy working to survive that you don't have time to raise your profile in a meaningful way—because that's the only thing that will give you long-term brand security.

As of this writing, I charge $6,000 for a half-day strategy session with clients. That's a far cry from the early days of my business. It's the result of getting clear on the value I can bring; building my brand to attract the right kind of clients (who would be happy to work with me, even at a premium price point); and being confident enough to name that price and stand firm on it.

Author Kevin Kruse learned a lesson about understanding one's own value a number of years ago, from an unexpected source: someone he was trying to hire as a speaker. At the time, Kruse was running a nonprofit life-sciences association, and his job was to organize the annual convention. "The board really wanted this one specific guy who was an expert on creativity" as the keynote speaker, he recalls. Even though Kruse had a budget of $30,000 to offer for the keynote address alone, he wasn't sure he could land the speaker, a *New York Times* best-selling author with an Ivy League doctorate and a heavy media presence.

But when he called, the author quoted a shockingly low fee: only $3,000. "From the outside," says Kruse, "it looked like he had all the signs of success and credibility, and we would have gladly paid literally ten times his asking price." As it was, Kruse wondered if the author's low fee scared a lot of people away, thinking he must be an inexperienced beginner on stage.

The speaker may have simply been clueless about market rates for his craft. But it's also possible he lacked the confidence to value himself appropriately.

Think about it: when something is simple for us, we often assume it must be easy for everyone else, notes Jason Van Orden, who runs the popular podcast and online training program *Internet Business Mastery*. If you're a golf instructor, for instance, the proper hand grip may be obvious to you. But by showing it to someone else, says Van Orden, you've saved them "maybe months of frustration and trying to figure it out, and you've just boiled it down into three lessons for them."

I became more confident raising my rates for two key reasons. First, I constantly upgraded my skills and reputation. I knew that I could safely charge more in the marketplace when I started blogging for the *Huffington Post* and, later, *Harvard Business Review*, because I'd be perceived as more of an expert. Second, I gained more clarity about what others were charging, which gave me confidence that my rates weren't out of line with the mainstream, and that I could even safely increase them. That's one of the reasons building relationships with other professionals in your field is worthwhile, so you can compare notes and make sure you're not undervaluing yourself.

Gaining the confidence to charge what you're worth is a common problem among new entrepreneurs. But it's vital that you do whatever it takes to overcome it—be it hiring a personal coach, finding a mentor, or getting involved with a mastermind group or professional association where you can develop a better sense of pricing in your market.

Focus on Metrics That Count

Social media is useful as a way to amplify your message and as a form of social proof to impress prospective publishers and the like. But as we've seen, it's extremely challenging to mobilize an audience through social media; you don't own the relationship, and you never know if someone is actually going to see your post or tweet. Yet it's often talked about as a panacea for brand building. When Natalie Sisson—now a successful online entrepreneur who brings in more than $250,000 per year—thinks about her early mistakes, this is the one she regrets.

More than a decade ago, when she launched her business, she became fascinated by the nascent social media scene. "Because I had no business model and no earnings or income, I was spending eight hours a day just communicating with people [online] and being in forums, looking at blogs, commenting on other blogs, and all those things that you do," she says. "That would be the only thing I'd do over . . . I would have liked to have funneled more of [that energy] into an email list and an offering."

Sisson learned that, while being active online gives the *appearance* of doing the right thing for your business, it may not be enough to keep you afloat. Sure, you're posting on sites, growing a following, and building goodwill, and those are important. But Jenny Blake, the author of *Pivot*, likes to draw a distinction between direct and indirect income-generating activities. She sees a lot of newer entrepreneurs who devote an inordinate amount of time to building their website or their Twitter following or designing their newsletter or logo.

"Those are great, but indirect," she says. They look like productive work, and may be in the long run, but they won't help pay the bills today.

Michael Parrish DuDell, author of *Shark Tank: Jump Start Your Business* (the television show *Shark Tank*'s official advice book), thinks of it as a division between long- and short-term concerns, or what he terms a "mind share play" and a "market share play." The former—activities such as appearing in the media—builds his reputation over the long term; appearing on Fox News or CNN likely won't bring in clients tomorrow, but appearing on major television networks will reinforce his credibility. A "market share play," on the other hand, is what keeps his business funded in the present. "With something like consulting, where maybe I'm making a lot of money, people [outside the client] aren't seeing the work that I'm doing," he says. To succeed over time, you need both types of activities.

Try This:

In thinking about what metrics really count for you, ask yourself the following questions:

- How much time per week, or per day, are you spending on social media? What's the return you hope to get, and how are you quantifying it? Is it worth it?

- What are your own "mind share" and "market share" plays? Make a list of each. How are you allocating your time, and does this feel like the right balance?

Overcome Resistance

Some professionals may hesitate to monetize because they fear the audience reaction. Indeed, people who are used to getting something for free may well rebel once you ask them to start paying. That's what happened to Andrew Warner. A successful entrepreneur, Warner and his brother built a multimillion-dollar online greeting card business. "I felt like I was invincible," he recalls, and assumed his next venture, a foray into online invitations, would be an even bigger hit. But it didn't work out that way. "I ended up spending hundreds of thousands of dollars on this idea that really didn't turn into gold. It turned into mud," he says.

Looking for answers, he decided to reach out to other business owners: "I said, 'I want to learn from as many entrepreneurs as I can how to build a business and never make this mistake again.'" He recorded the interviews on Skype and, in 2008, launched *Mixergy*, a website and video podcast where he compiled them. For a couple of years, he offered them all for free. But eventually, Warner was devoting so much time to the enterprise—including hiring a staff to help him with editing and doing pre-interviews of his guests—that he decided to start charging $25 per month for access.

As soon as he did, he heard about it. "People were posting publicly that I shouldn't be charging, and people were emailing me and saying 'What are you doing?'" he recalls. The feedback stung. "I felt hurt that my audience didn't like me as much." But charging an access fee enabled him to keep investing the time in creating the site, which now contains more than twelve hundred interviews. "If you do something that matters, some people are going to dislike you," he says. "Some people are going to disagree with you. It's not an indication that you're on the wrong track."

Try This:

As you start psyching yourself up to monetize, it's worth considering the following:

- Get clear on what it costs you to share your work with others. Are there recording or editing expenses? Website hosting fees? The cost of your time? The first step is to understand what you're already putting in, so you can determine what breakeven (and beyond) would look like.

- Think about various pricing models. Can you continue to offer some material for free, for those who genuinely can't pay, while offering exclusive paid content to your super-fans?

- Brace for criticism. You'll inevitably face some blowback, but don't take the outliers too seriously. If 90 percent of your audience is upset, you may want to reconsider. But if three people send you churlish emails, try to put it out of your head.

Strike the Right Balance

Asking your audience for money before you've built up a relationship and trust is doomed to failure. But delaying too long can be just as damaging. It's important to get the timing right. "I think people wait too long to sell to their audience," says Van Orden, who has trained more than seven thousand online entrepreneurs. "We try to get our students to make their first money from selling something they created as soon as possible. Even if that's just one sale . . . We know that from the moment they make their first $10, $5, $100, whatever, their confidence goes through the roof."

It can be awkward—very awkward—to ask for the first sale. But it's necessary. Michael Bungay Stanier, author of *The Coaching Habit* and the proprietor of a successful training firm, recalls his early days: "When I started coaching, I did a lot of pro bono stuff because I was just trying to get experience. But I think I was charging people around $200 for four one-hour calls per month." He quickly found himself exhausted and decided to raise his rates to avoid burnout.

"At a really tactical level, it's just practice," he says, referring to getting comfortable quoting your fee. "Somebody once said to me, 'Your going rate should be 'fear plus 10 percent'.' I love that, because it's like, what's the level you're comfortable saying: $1,000? All right, add 10 percent, so it's $1,100. Now, go and say that in front of a mirror twenty times. You'll feel like an idiot, but what happens is the phrase loses some of its power."

Jenny Blake agrees. You may well need the income, so you can't quote sky-high fees with impunity. But you can steadily and incrementally increase them until you feel you're earning what you deserve. "I still have one client paying me $500 a month because he's grandfathered in after years of working together," she says. "But the next time you pitch to a client, it's $850, and the next time, $1,000." If you hit a level where clients start to resist, you can consider freezing or reducing your rates until you've built up other income streams or increased your reputation in some other way (landing a marquee client, starting to write for a prominent publication) that may justify a higher fee.

Even with a small audience, monetization is possible. "If you've got a hundred people on an email list, you should be selling something to those people," says Van Orden. "Survey them and figure it out. The truth is, you only need one ideal [customer] to make some money. I also tell people that especially if you've made it to a thousand people on an email list and you're not selling anything, you're leaving money on the table, for sure."

If you're clear on your ideal audience and present them with relevant offers, he says, "there's just no reason that a three-thousand-person list that's well targeted shouldn't be making somebody $100,000 or more off their knowledge and their ideas."

For my part, I waited too long to start diversifying my revenue streams and monetizing my email list. For years, I focused almost exclusively on building my brand (through blogging, speaking for free, and writing books), and earning money from corporate gigs (consulting and, eventually, paid talks). That earned me a good living.

But it wasn't until I got serious about building my email list and growing my audience that I realized exactly how much revenue I was forsaking. In 2015, when I first started to share affiliate offers with my audience, I earned an additional $20,000—not too shabby for a few messages and webinars I offered throughout the year. In 2016, I earned well over six figures from my list alone.

You can't come from nowhere and immediately start raking in tens of thousands of dollars. Trust is the essential ingredient, and you need to show your audience that you're knowledgeable and put your relationship with them first, before any potential financial gain.

But Van Orden is right. Too many professionals, including myself, err on the side of caution and are too slow to sell. We delay sharing offers with our audience because of concern that we'll face blowback or have others question our integrity. But if you stand behind the resources you're offering, that attitude is doing your audience a disservice. It's denying them access to tools or services that can help them, and denying yourself the opportunity to build a business that's truly sustainable.

Once you've gained the courage to start monetizing your expertise, you'll want to consider bumping up your reputation and earnings by becoming a coach or consultant—the topic of the next chapter.

Try This:

Now it's time to get more specific with your plans to set your fees. Ask yourself:

- What's the going rate that others in your field are charging? If you don't know, start researching online and asking friends and colleagues. You can't price yourself fairly if you don't know what the range is.

- Based on your knowledge and skills, how do you want to position yourself? Are you a beginner, eager to get clients and experience? Or are you a seasoned pro looking to expand a new income stream? Once you understand the market, you can price yourself according to the brand you want to create in the marketplace.

- Practice stating your rate, whether it's in mock interviews with your friends or in the mirror. You won't get others to accept your fees unless you believe you're worth it yourself.

CHAPTER 4

Become a Coach or a Consultant

Stories of internet millionaires have become folklore in our culture, so it may seem almost old-fashioned to propose making money through hands-on coaching or consulting work. But even if you eventually aspire to leverage your talents online, I'll argue that in order to understand your audience's needs—and to be sure your advice really works—it's important to begin with traditional (often in-person) consulting activities, whether that's working one-on-one with an executive to help her develop leadership skills, crafting a company's social media plan, advising a business on implementing its new HR policy, or any other area in which you have expertise.

If you're just launching your entrepreneurial career, coaching or consulting offers the perfect sidestream income. They're an almost zero-cost way to launch your business and bring in immediate revenue, because they require no overhead beyond a roof over your head and a laptop. These activities serve as a laboratory where you can test and refine your ideas before bringing them to a wider stage, gain more knowledge, and cultivate a small cadre of passionate advocates who can help spread your message. What's more, you directly see the impact you're having, providing hands-on help to people who need it.

In this chapter, we'll explore ways to develop your initial network and spread the word about your services; grow that network exponentially; make a substantive contribution; expand your practice; systematize your approach; generate revenue with a premium offering; and, eventually, license your intellectual property.

Develop Your Initial Market

When Michael Parrish DuDell, author of the *Shark Tank* book, launched his consultancy, he wasn't sure he'd be successful. The focus of his business had always been content creation, but he had never sold anything before and wasn't sure if he could. He set a punishing goal for himself: if he couldn't close at least one client in thirty days, he'd shut down the business. "There's no do-overs, no retries," he recalls. "If I can't do it, I go out of business, and I work for somebody else. End of story."

He knew he thrived under pressure, and he kept focused. "I woke up every day with a single thought: 'You have to close, you have to close.' By the end of the first month, I had closed three big clients. I remember when I closed my first deal . . . I had to be cool on the phone, because you have to sort of be professional, but the second I got off the phone, I just sat there: *You just closed a $25,000 deal.*"

Of course, those deals didn't just materialize out of nowhere. He had to relentlessly seek them out, and that meant doing something that many nascent entrepreneurs find terrifying: *asking for the sale*. "I reached out to my network and told them what I was doing," DuDell says. "I think this is a problem, that people feel uncomfortable just stating what they're doing." They may still be unsure of their skills or their focus area, and they don't want to risk embarrassing themselves in front of their friends and colleagues. But that's the only way to get business initially.

Consulting, says DuDell, was "the lowest-hanging fruit, something that I could easily execute, and a small proof point along my journey that would teach me that I could run a business. It didn't require any capital; it didn't require any huge life sacrifices. I could do this in a safe space that would give me the room I needed to see if it worked and then go from there."

When I started my consulting business, I also tapped my preexisting network. Almost always, that's where your first business will come from, because those are the people who like you and trust you enough to do business with you, even though you may not have a track record in consulting.

Looking back, I should have written out a list of potential clients already in my network, and called or personally emailed each of them to suggest a meeting and see how I could help them—much like DuDell's approach. But even with my haphazard launch—simply sending out a blast email to my contacts letting them know I was going out on my own—I managed to land several marquee clients within two months.

Without exception, they were past colleagues who were now in positions where they had hiring authority, and I was able to benefit immediately from the social proof of consulting for clients like Yale University and the US National Park Service.

Try This:

As you're launching your consulting practice (or sideline), ask yourself:

- Have you directly reached out—individually, not via blast email—to all your friends and colleagues, telling them about your work and asking if they know anyone who might need your services? If not, do it now.

- Think about people you've worked with in the past who may have migrated to new companies, or old colleagues or contacts from college, grad school, sports teams, professional associations, or the like. Who is in a position where they could conceivably hire you? Start your outreach there.

Grow Your Network

DuDell tapped his existing network for business. But what if you don't have a network that can hire you? One way is to ask friends (or friends of friends) for introductions. It's a longer road, because you need to build relationships with your new contacts; you almost certainly won't close a deal within a month, as DuDell did when he launched. But over time, your new connections may pay off.

It's worthwhile to get specific about the type of people you'd like to meet; your friends need to be able to visualize who would be a good introduction for you. For instance, you could say, "I'd love to consult for Google one day. Do you know anyone who works there that you might be able to introduce me to?" Or you could sort by title and tell your friends, "I'm interested in making connections with anyone you know who is a vice president of human resources. Do you know anyone with that role?"

Lastly, you can also use LinkedIn to speed up this process; you can scour your friends' contacts to see if there's a specific person you'd like an introduction to. People's level of closeness to their LinkedIn contacts varies; be prepared for them to say they don't actually know the person well, or at all. But if they are good friends with that person, they may well be willing to make a personal introduction.

Michael Bungay Stanier, the author of *The Coaching Habit*, hardly knew anyone when he moved to Toronto, and he asked his friends for help. Melissa knew Lindsay, who knew David, who knew Nancy, an HR executive at a local bank. After this circuitous chain of introductions, Bungay Stanier invited Nancy to attend one of his workshops, and at lunchtime, he recalls, "She pulls me aside and says, 'Brilliant. You know what, I was just about to sign a contract with a different vendor, but I've decided I want you to do our coaching program. Can you give me a contract by tomorrow . . . [and] can you invoice us for $100,000?'" It was four degrees of separation, but the relationship Bungay Stanier developed with Nancy proved invaluable.

What if you don't have *any* friends or contacts who can be helpful to your business? In that case, start speaking for free, even in unlikely places.

Todd Herman grew up as a sports fanatic in Western Canada. He was the volunteer coach of a high school football team and often spoke to his students about overcoming internal obstacles and winning "the mental game." His approach was popular, so parents started asking him to do one-on-one coaching for their kids. He enjoyed the work, and to grow his clientele, he started calling local youth sports associations to see if they'd have him as a speaker, but he had one important request. "I'll come up and give a talk for free," he'd tell them. "But one parent for each of the kids has to be there." Otherwise, he knew the buyers of his service would never hear his message.

He'd make an explicit ask for speaking referrals: "I'd love it if any of you have another kid that isn't here tonight, or if you have a relationship with another association or team, to come and talk to me, and I'd love to set something up." Because the talks were free, the uptake was huge: "I did sixty-eight speeches in ninety days," he recalls.

The talks were prime marketing for his youth-coaching business. But they also created another opportunity he'd never imagined: providing the same services to adults. "I was in front of people I could have never reached in another medium," he says. "Really influential individuals—the head of a major NHL [National Hockey League] hockey team that happened to be there to support his son who was playing, so I started talking to him."

Herman soon began coaching NHL players and found that the prestige afforded him entry into new realms. Prominent professional sports players, jazzed about their mental toughness coach, began mentioning him to others in their social circle.

His lectures to youth sports groups continued to pay surprising dividends. One soccer dad approached him after only his second talk. "Todd, I absolutely love the message you were talking about, and I can totally see how this is going to help my daughter," he said. But he was also a high-level official in the Canadian government and was having a problem with another official.

"He's running roughshod over the entire crew," the official told Herman, "and we're really struggling with communication and leadership issues, plus there's a culture problem. Could you come in?" When Herman agreed, an entire new wing of his coaching business was launched, and with the Canadian government as his first client, he immediately garnered massive social proof he could leverage into work with other prominent organizations.

Like Herman, I spoke extensively for free when I first started my business—for local civic groups, the Chamber of Commerce, nonprofit incubators, and more. None of these were paid; my reward was "exposure" and perhaps a few email addresses if people signed up to join my list. That's a bad bargain for experienced speakers, but in the early days of your business, it's a critical way to gain credibility, get known, and make connections. If you can turn a free hour-long talk into a consulting engagement worth tens of thousands of dollars, it's worth it.

In chapter 5, we'll discuss how to develop a paid speaking business. But when you're first starting out, giving free talks is an ideal way to market your coaching or consulting services and get the onstage experience you need in order to deserve being paid later on.

Try This:

As you're considering ways to grow your network, ask yourself:

- Have you reached out to your friends and colleagues to ask if they know people in your target city and/or industry? See if they're willing to introduce you.

- Make a list of nonprofit, civic, or professional associations where you could volunteer to speak. If the audience members themselves aren't potential buyers of your service, be clear on how you can bridge the gap to reach buyers (like Todd Herman's request that parents be present for his talks). Reach out to at least three this week.

Make a Substantive Contribution

Of course, once you're inside an organization as a consultant or coach, you need to contribute unique insights. That, ultimately, is what justifies your fee, though it can sometimes be hard to feel confident expressing a different or contrarian perspective. "Early on in my career," recalls executive coach Alisa Cohn, "I would have an inkling of something, and I wouldn't share it."

In one instance, one company was taking over another, and her client was being asked to run it. Cohn says, "It turned out he was being put into a position where he couldn't succeed, but everybody was paying lip service to the idea that 'No really, it'll be OK,' including him. But I didn't think it would be OK, and it was not OK. I wish I had been more clear and stronger in my point of view."

She learned from the experience, and today, directness has become one of the cornerstones of her coaching work. She describes the critical difference between "inquiry" and "advocacy." Good coaches balance the need to draw out the facts and the client's perspective through asking questions (inquiry) with sharing their own opinion, based on their knowledge and experience (advocacy). Getting that equation right enables you to make a genuine contribution to a client and give them their money's worth.

Just as it takes a while for a musician or writer to find a "voice," it's the same for consultants and coaches. Early on, you may not be sure what's distinctive about your approach. But with time and practice (it's a good idea to make friends your initial pro bono guinea pig clients), you'll begin to understand what makes you unique. Like Cohn, I've learned that "playing it safe" by tamping down your opinions isn't helpful to clients. The entire reason they're seeking an outside perspective is because they probably have too many yes-men in their organization, and they need a different point of view.

In one instance, I'd been consulting with a prominent C-level executive for about eighteen months. We'd reached an inflection point in the engagement where he needed to choose a course of action and simply wasn't willing to make a call. I pressed him during our meeting and was even more fervent in my follow-up memo: this failure to decide risked jettisoning everything he was working toward. It was tough love, and he let several of my follow-up emails go unanswered. I was convinced I wouldn't hear from him again. But four months later, he invited me back.

Since then, I've been repeatedly convinced he would cancel our engagement because I push so forcefully against ideas that I think would be damaging for him. Some clients probably would call things off. But the enlightened ones realize that someone who's willing to tell them the truth, regardless of the consequences, is what they need most. My commitment isn't to please my clients; it's to help them, which I consider a higher calling.

Indeed, as I gained consulting and coaching experience, I felt much freer to be frank, joke about situations, and just be myself, rather than feeling as if there was a Platonic idea of a consultant I somehow needed to emulate. To my surprise—though it shouldn't have been—I discovered that clients relish working with a consultant who seems real.

In a world where far too many people try to hew to the safe path, smart clients appreciate it when they understand they're being dealt with straight and that you're willing to raise even challenging topics or unpopular opinions.

Expand Your Practice

Once you've begun to develop a coaching or consulting practice, referrals sometimes happen organically, as with the professional hockey players referring Herman to their friends and teammates. But a smart practitioner also proactively seeks out referral business and other ways to leverage a one-to-one relationship into something more.

"Once I'm in an organization," says Cohn, "I tend to talk to a lot of folks in the company [while respecting confidentiality where needed]. It helps me help them, because I get a sense of what's on the minds of people at all levels of the organization, and get in touch with the culture of the organization," so she can provide more insightful advice to the senior leaders who have hired her.

But making those connections also serves a valuable networking and business development purpose. Cohn says, "As I get to know people and become trusted, they're like, 'Hey, I want some of that [coaching].' So then they start asking for it, or the company will see how I can be useful in a larger group setting. So that's a way I expand my reach within the organization, and I'll also ask for referrals from CEO clients."

Another way to think about growing your practice is to expand into group coaching work. Of course, that's a secondary step: if you can't get one client, you're going to have a hard time landing ten. But once you've gained some experience and an initial base of clients, it can be an interesting and lucrative option.

When Michael Port's first book, *Book Yourself Solid*—a success manual for coaches and consultants—became a best-seller in 2006, he suddenly had a massive new audience. Before that, he'd just focused on building a one-to-one coaching business. But now, with seven thousand new opt-ins to his email list on launch day alone, he suddenly had the scale to build a group coaching program.

Initially, he created a teleseminar series, because at the time, most internet connections weren't robust enough to support video-based webinars. The three-month program, with weekly calls, cost $1,200, and demand was strong. "I had fifty people in the program, and then seventy people in the program, and it started growing from there," he says.

He began experimenting with the model, shifting to a year-long mentoring program that initially cost $8,000 per person, which entitled them to several training calls a month, plus three three-day retreats each year. He had an initial cohort of forty participants, and even as he increased the price point—first to $10,000 per year, and then $12,000—he was able to draw between 150 and 250 mentees each year. But participants found the travel costs pricey, and Port discovered that executing large, live events was both costly and stressful.

Even for popular, money-making programs, it's important to question assumptions periodically and explore new models that may be more fun or gratifying. That's why, in 2015, Port shifted the model of his mentorship program dramatically. He eliminated the multiday, live events and slashed the price for participation in his mentoring program. Instead of $1,000 per month, he's now charging only $89; participants get access to nine training calls per month, one conducted by Port and the others by his trained associates. At the time of our interview, shortly after the program's relaunch, he was up to five hundred participants, with plans to hit a thousand by the end of the year.

Right now, the new version is bringing in less money than his previous mentorship program. But it's with a fraction of the effort for Port, and over time, the lower price point may well draw in enough new participants to make up the difference. That's why, in planning your mix of offerings, it's important to consider both revenue and scale. "I made more money with fewer people at [the $12,000 price point], but I consider that a bad thing," says Port. "I want more people out in the world [listening to his message], not fewer people out in the world."

Try This:

As you think about how you can expand the referrals you receive from your existing clients, it's worth considering the following questions:

- Do you specifically *ask* for referrals? If not, reach out to at least one satisfied customer this week and ask if they know of other people or organizations that might benefit from your help.

- Looking at your existing clients, are there other departments or field offices where your services might be needed? Talk to your existing clients and see if they would be willing to make an introduction.

Systematize Your Approach

You can grow your coaching or consulting business by seeking referrals or by pursuing group models. But you also scale it by systematizing your approach. That's what John Jantsch eventually did with his Kansas City marketing consultancy, though when he started it in 1988, he had no system at all. "I wouldn't even say there was any strategy involved," he recalls. "It was pretty much, 'What do you need? Sure, we'll do that.'"

But he worked hard, his business grew, and eventually— unless he wanted to add more staff and take on more over- head—he couldn't serve any more clients. That was a risky proposition, however, because he couldn't really raise his rates; the small business clients he loved to help often had minimal marketing budgets.

That's when he started thinking about how to provide his con- sulting more efficiently. "It's difficult to buy marketing solutions in a comprehensive way," he says. "There's lots of people sell- ing social media expertise. There are people selling SEO [search engine optimization], blogging, and all the various components. But there really wasn't anybody that said, 'Here's marketing as a system. We're going to install a system.'" What if he could do just that?

So he started to write down his ideas about the foundational principles of marketing for small businesses, things like "figur- ing out who your ideal client is, what you can bring to the world that's remarkable, that essentially makes the competition irrele- vant." And once the foundation was built, his system helped small businesses figure out, "What are the channels that we're going to generate leads in and how are we going to convert those leads?"

In the beginning, he'd mail three-ring binders with two hun- dred pages of printed sheets to his clients. Before long, the new system—which he called Duct Tape Marketing—became a hit, especially when he started sharing his insights on the internet as one of the first marketing bloggers.

Selling the *system*, instead of providing ad hoc, one-off con- sulting, was a revelation for Jantsch. He says, "There were cer- tain elements where you realize, 'Well, everybody needs these three things, and if we go in and do our research [with clients], our discovery process, and our intake in the same way, we'll get better results.' What I found is that we got much more efficient doing it, and consequently, much more profitable." He was also able to shift to a recurring monthly retainer model, rather than project or hourly consulting work. He says, "It became apparent to me this was a much more stable way to do it ... The longer I worked with a client, the more profitable I got."

His system, with its catchy name, became a crucial branding differentiator, as well. "They weren't buying me anymore," he says, and he no longer had to compete with other marketing consultants. "It was, 'I want that system. I want that approach. I want that methodology.'" Today, Duct Tape Marketing is a multimillion-dollar brand and a behemoth in the small business consulting marketplace.

Try This:

As you consider how to systematize your practice, ask yourself:

- Were there common elements in your last three to five client engagements? What steps did you need to go through with each client?

- Write down the most common, standardized approach to your work. Of course, there will be small variations for every client. But what are the key elements everyone needs? What pieces are mandatory for success? This can become the root of your own system.

Generate Revenue with a Premium Offering

When you're starting a side business or an entrepreneurial venture, it may feel less risky to start small—maybe sell an online course for $50 or publish an ebook for $2.99. Those can be fine options for additional revenue once you've built an audience, and we'll discuss online course creation in more depth in chapter 9. But aiming for low-dollar, high-volume sales almost certainly won't support you when you're first starting out. Instead, aim higher.

"A lot of people think, 'Oh, maybe I should just start with inexpensive stuff where there's little commitment, little involvement, and then move my way up,'" says Selena Soo, the publicity and business development strategist. "I think it's actually better to launch with a premium offering." Because I was so hesitant to alienate customers when I launched my business and wasn't sure what to charge anyway, I took the traditional route and accepted even very small projects. But Soo's path was smarter.

She began her career in the nonprofit world, earning $42,000 per year—a challenge in pricey New York City.[1] Tired of the low pay and grueling hours, she rebooted with an MBA and realized, in the process, that premium pricing would be her path to success. Upon graduation, when she launched her own business, her initial offering was a $5,000, six-month coaching program. "With the $5,000 package, you could easily create a six-figure business because basically you just need to get ten clients to pay you $5,000, and then in half a year, you've made $50,000," she says. "Then all you need is for those who bought to renew, or you find new people."

That might sound daunting, but she'd taken steps beforehand to build her bona fides and connections. Using her knowledge of public relations, she built meaningful relationships with influencers like online entrepreneurs Ramit Sethi and Marie Forleo by helping them win publicity. They, in turn, became her supporters, providing testimonials and social proof (i.e., credibility by association).

With those testimonials as a starting point, she also began guest blogging for established industry players and appearing on their podcasts, which led to significant visibility. By tapping her growing database of contacts for client referrals, she was able to fill the slots in her program and eventually shifted into an even pricier model, an annual mastermind program that cost more than $20,000.

There were brand benefits to her positioning, as well. "When you have a premium program, you're going to be working with high-end, premium people," she says. "These people also had their own audiences," who noticed the affiliation with Soo and became intrigued. "You planted that seed, so that people think, *I want to work with that person [Soo] one day.*"

Try This:

As you consider ways to break into the high end, ask yourself:

- What high-ticket service could you realistically offer? Write out a description that includes all the specifics. Who is your ideal client? What is the price point of your offering? What will they get in return? What is the duration? Why will it appeal to them? Why should they choose to work with you, rather than someone else? Answering these questions—and seeing where there are holes—can be an enormously helpful exercise in clarifying your value proposition and understanding what your target audience desires.

- What skills do you have that you could leverage to help influencers in your industry? Write down one to three people you could realistically assist in some way. It's important to think carefully, because some forms of "help" are actually burdensome to the recipient, like writing them to ask, "How can I help you?" when they don't know who you are. But targeted, high-value assistance—such as Soo generating public relations opportunities, or Derek Halpern providing detailed website audits—may allow you to stand out from the crowd.

License Your Intellectual Property

Every coach or consultant who has run themselves ragged delivering programs to clients has lamented, *why can't I clone myself?* Licensing—a process in which others pay you to use the intellectual property you've created, such as coaching techniques or materials—allows you to do just that. It's only possible once you've built a substantial enough group of satisfied clients and interested followers. But once you do, the revenue-generation possibilities are substantial.

As consultant Andrew Sobel, who licenses his sales and relationship-building methodology internationally, puts it: "Step one is, prove your concept with your own clients. If you haven't built a significant personal consulting business around your product, frankly, if you haven't built a very, very strong six- or seven- or even eight-figure practice around it, I'm not sure it's licensable."

It makes sense: if anyone is going to pay to learn your methodology, they want proof that it works and that the market values it so they can recoup their investment. Step two, says Sobel, is to "start with your own clients and see if you can sell programs to them," where you're getting an intellectual property licensing fee and training their trainers. Once you have those two proof points, licensing could be a good possibility for you.

On the other hand, if you've laid the groundwork, sometimes opportunities do just present themselves. Jantsch published *Duct Tape Marketing* in 2007, and within a few years, his passionate fan base was literally begging for the training. Jantsch recalls receiving phone calls from people telling him, "'I want to be a Duct Tape Marketing consultant.' I was like, 'Oh, I guess I better create a licensing program.'"

Much more difficult—but clearly not impossible—was William Arruda's licensing strategy. Arruda was working as a corporate brand manager for IBM when he discovered the concept of personal branding. He loved his job, but after reading Tom Peters' now-famous *Fast Company* cover story on the topic ("The Brand Called You," from 1997), he became inspired.[2]

He quit his job in 2001 to become a full-time personal brand coach and expected the clients to pour in. To his surprise (and mounting terror), they did not. "Nobody knew what [personal brand coaching] was, and fewer people wanted to buy it," he recalls.

But his lack of clients did give him one gift: plenty of time. During his initial two years in business, he says, "I was able to take everything I knew about branding and do a ton of research and create a methodology, and then try that methodology out for free, frankly, with executives to see what worked and what didn't, so I could refine it."

Arruda had a realization: in order to win clients, he needed to raise overall customer awareness of personal branding. He had an asset—his finely honed intellectual property—that he could leverage. What if he used it to train aspiring personal branding coaches? On the one hand, he was creating his own competition. But on the other, he desperately craved a like-minded community and believed that since personal branding was such a nascent field, the more people promoting the concept, the better for everyone. "I was lonely," Arruda says, "and there was nobody to talk to about personal branding but me . . . I thought, 'How do I get colleagues?' And I thought about a certification program. By doing that, I was able to amplify the message."

Most people without a preexisting following or at least a robust business model would have trouble interesting others in a licensing program. But Arruda short-circuited the typical process by developing his thorough methodology early on in what came to be a hot field. He launched his licensing program in 2003.

"What I did was target early adopters in the careers industry," he recalls. "It wasn't even executive coaches back then. It was really people who used to be résumé writers and career counselors, and this essentially gave them a new tool in their toolkit and a new vernacular and a new way of looking at what they do."

Starting a Licensing Program

Licensing your material is surprisingly different from doing the work yourself. "It was a real learning experience," says Arruda. "One of the benefits of having a licensing program is you get crystal clear about your methodology because now it's not just you using it. It needs to be so easy to use and turnkey that you really start to refine your process."

But it's not just about honing the techniques: it's also creating a shared worldview. Jantsch recommends that anyone who wants to license their methodology should make a point of creating unique names for your ideas, such as "the Marketing Hourglass," his trademarked term for what is more commonly known as the "marketing funnel," which describes the process of how customers come to know about you and eventually buy from you. "I know that can be really cliché, and you can be over the top with it," Jantsch admits. But a little goes a long way. He says, "When people start reading your stuff or start following you, they have a common language." That creates a sense of community cohesion and shared ideas and values.

Once you've decided to launch, you need to answer a critical question up front: Is your certification good forever, or must it be renewed each year? *Book Yourself Solid* author Port, who charges $20,000 for the license, takes the former approach. With an annual renewal, he was concerned that "people would have to reevaluate every year if they want to keep it, and I don't want that," he says. "I want to have a community that people feel they're in forever." Each month, he holds some form of professional development activity for all licensees, though, of course, participation is optional.

Jantsch and Arruda favor annual certification, however, because they believe it's easier to keep licensees up to date on changing best practices and to provide an out in case of an unruly participant who might be damaging the brand. Jantsch, for instance, charges $10,000 for the initial certification and a $2,500 annual recertification fee after that, which includes ongoing training and access to the community. "It's like being part of an association," he says. The recertification process—submitting sample work that you've done with a client that year for evaluation—isn't incredibly onerous, he says, but it's enough to show that they're serious about quality control.

Keep in mind that your licensing program will likely change over time and evolve. Arruda started out licensing 5 people at a time; in 2015, he certified 192 people, and more than 1,000 have been licensed since the program's inception. You won't know up front what information your licensees most need, or what questions they'll have or pitfalls they'll face. "I don't think there's any way to very accurately go out and say, 'Here it is. It's done. It's perfect,'" says Jantsch.

Instead, "build it with some people that are likely candidates to want to buy it," says Jantsch. "Let them be a part of developing it. Let them have it for a really reduced price with the agreement that they're going to give you lots and lots of feedback."

In other words, pilot your licensing program before going too deep, and make sure you're creating a product the market actually wants. If so, licensing can be an enjoyable and lucrative way to spread your ideas. "Our message is being amplified by the number of people we certified, and all of the people they touch," says Arruda. "That's invaluable. It's something you would never be able to do on your own."

Managing the Risks

Your reputation is on the line when it comes to licensees who bear your official stamp of approval. What if someone goes rogue and adds in their own (potentially misguided) approach? What if they misrepresent you or mangle your methodology? What if they treat clients poorly and it reflects on you? Those are all valid concerns. But at a certain point, says Port, you have to let it go.

Port started certifying consultants in his Book Yourself Solid methodology in 2009. "People kept saying, 'Well, are you worried about watering down your brand?' At first I was like, 'Yeah, of course I'm worried about that.' Then I was like, 'Wait a minute, people are already using my stuff anyway. Why shouldn't I get paid for it? They're already out there teaching it, so I might as well actually train people to do it right and then represent that brand out in the world very well.'"

Jantsch, similarly, has reconciled himself to the fact that all he can do is provide quality training to his network of more than 110 licensees; he can't control everything. "There's only so much you can do, unless you just want to become a policing organization," he says.

One of the ways he avoids potential problems is creating a robust licensee community that can provide mutual support and set group norms. "We do an annual gathering of the network," he says. "We do bimonthly calls on specific subjects that I think they need to know about. My approach always was: *keep training, keep building the relationship.* Keep the members of the network close, and you probably mitigate a little bit of the risk of somebody just going out there and (a) either ripping you off; or (b) really causing damage to the brand."

A coaching or consulting program like those described in this chapter provides a great way to generate income and build your base of followers. That's when you'll find yourself in a good position to expand into other realms, like paid professional speaking.

Try This:

If you have a stream of others who are interested in learning your methodology, it may be time to launch a licensing program. Think about:

- What are the steps in your process? Break them down into small and discrete modules, preferably with unique and memorable names that will become associated with you and your approach.

- What's the best way to convey this knowledge? Will you do the training entirely online, or will there be an in-person component? How will you structure it? One intensive training over a week or a weekend? Multiple sessions over the course of a year? What will your version of continuing education look like?

- How much will you charge for certification? And does it last forever, or is there an annual renewal fee? How will you verify who is still in compliance (or not) with your approach?

CHAPTER 5

Build a Speaking Practice

I knew I needed to grow my consulting business, and speaking seemed like a great way to do it. I was comfortable onstage and enjoyed interacting with audiences. So early on in my career, I'd volunteer to speak for free to almost any group that would have me. I had "stretch goals," of course—like one regional Chamber of Commerce that held regular breakfast events attended by hundreds of business leaders. If I could only get in front of this group, I thought. So I prepared a handsome packet of information—a folder with my bio, information about my talks, and a DVD I'd paid well over $1,000 to have a professional film and edit.

When I called a couple of weeks later to make sure the Chamber staff had received my packet, to my surprise, they hadn't. The packet must have gotten lost. So I reassembled it and mailed it again. On my next follow-up call, I learned the truth. "No, we never got that," an assistant intoned. "Can you send it again?" It was a line—the one staffers fed to people they'd never heard of and deemed too insignificant even to consider. The office had simply thrown it out.

I learned a couple of valuable lessons that day. First, that I somehow had to become better known, so I would never be dismissed that way again. And second, I began to understand what I've come to call Clark's Law of Professional Speaking:

1. At first, no one is interested in having you speak.

2. Then, they're interested if you'll speak for free.

3. Eventually, they're interested if they can get you cheap.

4. Finally, they're intent on having you and they'll pay you what you're worth.

If you hope to build a successful paid speaking practice, it's essential to understand where you are in this progression so you can calibrate your activities and your speaking fees accordingly. With this Chamber of Commerce group, I was clearly at step one.

I committed myself over the next few years to building my brand so that I could move up the ladder. In this chapter we'll look at some of the things I learned from my experience and from the other professional speakers I interviewed, including the ins and outs of finding your first speaking gigs; the benefits of speaking for free; deciding when to ask for a fee, and how much; how to master outbound marketing; and how to expand your network and monetize in other ways.

Find Your First Speaking Gigs

I hear from a lot of people who are starting out as speakers. Almost invariably, one of their first questions is how to find a speakers' bureau to help them book engagements. Unfortunately, that's the wrong question.

A speakers' bureau—which assembles a database of speakers whom it represents, some exclusively and some nonexclusively—is generally hired by corporations or associations to help them find and book speakers for events. I've worked with a few, and they can be helpful. But here's the truth: until you can bring in engagements on your own, they are not remotely interested in you. They make their payroll through commissions (often a hefty 25 percent) booking the Hillary Clintons and Colin Powells of the world, not by placing you with $5,000 engagements.

Some newbies view bureaus as a panacea—that once you're chosen to be represented (which means that your picture is placed on their website), opportunities will magically fall into your lap. That simply doesn't happen. Even if you're able to work with bureaus, until you reach a certain threshold of price and popularity, they're not going to expend any energy marketing you. All of my dealings with bureaus have come as the result of their clients going to them, saying, "Can you get me Dorie Clark?" and them saying, "Sure." They found my website and emailed me from there, arranged the contract, and earned a few thousand dollars' commission from the client for a few minutes' effort. Not bad work if you can get it.

In short, finding a bureau shouldn't be your main concern early on. Only by landing gigs can you start to build enough of a following to get bureaus interested, should you want to work with one later on. Banks don't really want to lend to you until you don't need their money, and similarly, speakers' bureaus don't really want to work with you until you have a solid enough marketing funnel that you can drive engagements without their help.

So if a speakers' bureau isn't going to help you find your first gigs, how do you find them yourself? The answer is, you don't. You actually have far more cachet when you avoid marketing yourself directly as a speaker. As Michael Parrish DuDell notes, the very act of marketing yourself diminishes your perceived credibility.

"Part of the allure of bringing in a noted speaker is that they are already established in their own field," he says. "By going and selling yourself as a speaker, you're discounting the value proposition of what you do. That's so backwards and crazy, but that's the reality." He found outbound marketing to be utterly ineffective and stopped trying years ago.

Instead, the secret is to use "inbound marketing" techniques—that is, attracting potential clients to you. You can do this in two ways. First, you can ask contacts who already know and like you to recommend you as a speaker. For instance, a client might recommend you as a speaker for the professional association she belongs to, or a friend who spoke at a conference last year may suggest you to the organizers.

Second, you can create content that will attract potential clients to you. For instance, I once wrote a blog post for *Harvard Business Review* about how to plan your professional development for the year. That article caught the attention of a professional association that asked if I could do a (paid) webinar on the topic, which I ran live for more than six hundred attendees, exposing me to an entirely new audience.

But most often, your first speaking engagements will be unpaid. The speakers I interviewed talked about the importance of speaking for free—widely—in the early days, so you can create initial momentum and a core audience of people who have seen you in action.

Try This:

As you're working to land your first speaking gigs, keep the following in mind:

- Make a list of clients who love your work. Reach out and ask if they're involved in professional associations they could refer you to, or if they attend conferences where they know the organizers. They may be willing to put in a good word on your behalf.

- If you have friends or colleagues who are speakers, ask them if they've spoken at any events lately for which they think you might be a fit. Approach this judiciously, because they're putting their reputation on the line for you. Only reach out to people with whom you're close, and be prepared to share a sample video with them so they can vet your speaking skills if they haven't already seen you onstage.

- Make a list of blogs you could write that tie in to your speeches. The goal is to create a marketing pipeline in which your content attracts interested customers who will reach out and ask, "Could you speak to our group about that?"

Speak for Free

Early on, speaking for free is a perfectly reasonable strategy. You can practice your skills and hone your craft, and it exposes you to audiences that may want to hire you for further engagements. "In the early days, I spoke for leads," recalls John Jantsch of Duct Tape Marketing fame. "I would go to whatever group asked me, if I thought there were prospects there, and I would give them a great educational experience. Undoubtedly, two or three people would come up and say, 'Can we talk about me hiring you?' To me, that was the payoff." The way he looked at it, if he could drum up consulting business, it wasn't a free speech at all. "That might have been a $100,000 speaking gig, with the right couple of engagements that came out of it."

Dan Schawbel, author of *Promote Yourself*, recalls one early free speaking gig at a college in Massachusetts. Nearly three years later, one of the attendees—who had by then graduated—got a job at a technology company that needed a speaker. She remembered Schawbel's talk and suggested bringing him in. He earned nearly $6,000 and it became his first paid talk.

When evaluating opportunities to speak for free, be clear on what criteria matter to you. You might want experience speaking in front of a group, period, in which case, it could be worthwhile to say yes to everybody. But if your time is limited, you can look at other benefits that might be useful to you.

"There are a lot of things you can get that are nonmonetary," says William Arruda, who speaks on personal branding. "Invite the head of HR to the program or bring your press connections to the program. Or ask someone to tape you for video you can use later. Or get everyone live-tweeting in the session, so that you're building your brand. Even for those [talks] where you're not being paid, come up with five ways that you can get something really valuable." It could be exposure to client prospects, as Jantsch described, recommendation letters or testimonials, or the opportunity to visit a special place or interact with people knowledgeable in your field.

If you are speaking for free or for a low rate, you can at least ask for travel expenses—and if they say no, you can then decide if the engagement is still worth it to you. Professional speaker Grant Baldwin sometimes asks if the organizers will pay for his family to accompany him on the trip. He once spoke at a discounted rate for a conference at a family-friendly resort "because we get a vacation out of it with my family, and my girls get to play at this amazing water park . . . The dollar amount may be less, but I'm still getting value out of it."

Very occasionally, I'll accept a speaking engagement simply because I'll get to see my friends who are also on the speaking circuit. For example, I agreed to speak at Social Media Marketing World, an annual conference in San Diego, despite the fact that it only covered my hotel expenses (I even had to pay for my own flight). But the organizers had brought together such a stellar lineup of other speakers that I was glad to go and see old friends like authors Michael Port and Mitch Joel. I also got to meet colleagues I'd long communicated with electronically but had never had the chance to meet in person, like authors Mark Schaefer and Joel Comm and podcaster John Lee Dumas. All this made the event worthwhile for me.

To be clear, even if you're speaking for free, finding gigs is rarely a quick process; it takes time to build your brand on the speaking circuit. But eventually the referrals from your free talks and inquiries that you receive because of your content start to pay off. Your name will become more recognizable, and then you'll begin winning your first paid talks.

Try This:

In the early days of your speaking business, ask yourself:

• What would make it worthwhile for you to speak at an event for free? Write up a list of at least half a dozen benefits you could get out of it (connecting with influencers, testimonial quotes, etc.). Think creatively.

When to Charge a Fee

Making the transition from a free speaker to a paid speaker is challenging. It's a psychological adjustment for you (you might find it hard to say, with a straight face, that you charge thousands of dollars an hour). And the people who booked you for free in the past may not be willing to start paying you; you'll likely need to cultivate new clients with budgets at their disposal.

The biggest factor for me in shifting from free to paid speaking work was the publication of my book *Reinventing You,* in 2013, which raised my profile and gave me an additional level of credibility. Before then, I'd never been paid more than a nominal fee of a couple hundred dollars to give a talk. After the book's publication, I began receiving more inquiries.

But even though I'd written a book, it still didn't occur to me that people would be willing to pay me. In the past, I often didn't even ask and assumed the engagement would have to be for free. Not surprisingly, event organizers were delighted to let me carry on with this assumption.

What finally changed my behavior, and got me to start asking for money, was something simple but powerful: inconvenience. I was approached just before the book's launch by a national association that was holding its annual conference. A colleague involved with the association had recommended me, and it wanted to know if I'd be willing to serve as the keynote speaker. It sounded like a great opportunity, and I was interested, but the date was wildly inconvenient for me. I theoretically *could* have made the date, but the travel and logistics were onerous.

So, to help with my cost-benefit analysis, I wrote back and asked about the budget. "We're just a nonprofit," the organizers told me, "so we don't really have a speakers' budget." Of course, almost all associations are nonprofits, and some are quite large. And—I know now—it's pure nonsense that it wouldn't have a speakers' budget for its keynote address for its national convention of nearly three thousand people. But at the time, I was a rookie, and many organizations will try to poor-mouth you. I might have normally taken the organizers at their word and agreed to speak pro bono. But it was simply too much of a hassle. So I wrote back and, with extreme regret, said I couldn't possibly speak for free.

Voila! Magically, that seemed to do the trick. The organizers shot back almost immediately: Could I do it for $5,000? I was astonished; I had actually believed them when they said they didn't have the money. It was a revelation how easy it was to negotiate—even when that's not what I was intending to do—an instantaneous $5,000 raise for myself. I had never received so much money for a talk; I agreed right away, because the travel inconvenience was definitely worth $5,000 to me.

That experience gave me the confidence to start asking for money, and I now charge $20,000 per talk. Of course, longtime best-selling authors like Malcolm Gladwell are reported to get up to $80,000 for a speech, and worldwide celebrities can bring in far more (as with Hillary Clinton's famous $225,000 speech to

Goldman Sachs). But it's still a tremendously lucrative activity and earns me a healthy six figures a year doing work I enjoy.

Know How Much to Charge

Here's a very general rule of thumb:

- Newbie speakers might earn $500–$2,500 for a talk.

- Beginning speakers or those just establishing their brand with a book might earn $5,000–$10,000.

- Those with books and other forms of "social proof" might draw $10,000–$20,000.

- Those who are very well known in their field, such as best-selling authors, can bring in $20,000–$35,000 per talk.

Celebrities and household names are in an entirely different stratosphere, earning $50,000–$300,000 per keynote. If you're in that category, put down this book immediately, call a speakers' bureau, tell them I sent you, and you can send me a commission.

But even for professionals who have established their rates, circumstances do vary. Nonprofit associations—despite the claims of the one that tried to boondoggle me—do have money. But it's often less than what corporations have at their disposal. State or regional associations operate on a more constrained budget than their national counterparts, for instance. That's why it's important, when you're initially taking in information about their request, to find out answers to questions like:

- How many people are expected to attend the talk?

- In general, who will be the attendees (title, level of seniority)?

- Where will it be located?

- What's the context of the event (conference, internal professional development, client appreciation event, etc.)?

- Will this be a keynote talk (generally forty-five to sixty minutes) or a breakout session?

Essentially, this will help you determine how important the event is and will give you a sense of how much they will value your participation. The more high profile—if it's for hundreds of senior executives at a resort in Aspen, for instance—the more budget they'll likely have available. Meanwhile, if it's a "lunch and learn" for a dozen interns at corporate headquarters, they may not be lying when they tell you they only have $500 to spend.

If the offer comes in below what you're accustomed to or what you'd like to be earning, you'll have to decide—based on some of the factors we identified earlier with regard to giving a free speech—if you're willing to take a reduced rate. Sometimes, the exposure or other benefits really will be worth it. Other times, it pays to stand firm. If the thought of taking three flights to earn $750 in Duluth in January makes you want to cry, don't do it. You should only accept speaking gigs where you feel excited about the opportunity.

Remember, too, that despite the often high hourly rates, for most professionals, speaking won't make you rich. "I'd guess that 95 percent of all professional speakers make less than $10,000 per speech," estimates speaker Chris Widener. "I'd say the sweet spot for most speakers is $6,000, plus or minus—probably $4,500–$7,500."[1] But especially when coupled with other forms of income generation, whether it's landing consulting clients or selling books or DVDs, it can become a powerful part of your portfolio career.

Try This:

As you begin to get comfortable charging for your talks, remember:

- When someone invites you to give a speech, *always* ask, "What's your speaker budget?" They may not have one, but you'll at least know the answer and can make an informed decision about whether you'd like to do the engagement.

- Have a number in mind for your preferred fee, based on your level of experience and the prominence of your brand. As you get to know other speakers (you may consider checking out groups like the National Speakers Association), you can see what others are charging and calibrate accordingly.

Master Outbound Marketing

When you're starting to speak for money, there are two initial credibility tools you must have to draw business: a website and a speaker demo video. Once you have those, you can think about actively presenting yourself to potential clients and asking for the sale. That's "outbound marketing," and as I've said, it rarely works early on. But it's not impossible.

Grant Baldwin, who has earned more than a million dollars directly from his professional speaking and has given more than 450 talks, took this approach at the start of his career. He started by filming his demo video "in a dark room with just a little handicam" that he set up to one side.

In my case, I paid a professional to film a talk I did (for free) at a local college. The lighting was great, but the videographer wasn't the sharpest strategic thinker: almost every shot she took of me had a backdrop of the snack table the students had laid out, so it looked like I was speaking at a bake sale. But it got me started. Over time, I began to speak at corporations that wanted to record the events; I always said yes, as long as I could have a copy for my own use, and those became my new video calling cards.

Armed with a website and a speaker video, you're now ready—if you choose—to reach out to potential clients. I made a few half-hearted efforts, as with the Chamber of Commerce, and gave up in disgust. But Baldwin figured out how to make it work, even without a best-selling book or blue-chip credentials.

In the beginning, he says, "it's a lot of guerrilla marketing." Baldwin had been speaking to high school and college students for little or no money, and wanted to break into corporate audiences, but he had few connections. So he turned to Google, searching terms like "real estate conference" and "realtors conference." You can find association meetings and conferences for virtually any industry segment.

Baldwin advises starting your search locally, as he did. He knew that without a strong brand, he wouldn't stand a chance at the national level. But he might be able to persuade someone who ran the local or state conference. "I vividly remember a couple of times printing off a list of all fifty states and making a list of all the different existing associations and conferences," he says. He'd find the executive director online and send them an inquiry.

"I had a database at one time of seven hundred or eight hundred contacts, and I would just try to email them once or twice a year," he says. "I didn't want to spam them; I didn't want to stalk them; I didn't want to be annoying." Baldwin says a lot of novice speakers find a promising conference and then send unsolicited emails that are pages long about how wonderful they are and why they'd make a good speaker, with a link to their site and video at the end. Says Baldwin: "Don't do that."

Instead, he did two important things. One, in his emails he erred on the side of brevity; and two, he made sure he followed up later.

"Often my sole goal was just to get them to reply," he says. He'd send a note along the lines of "Hey Dorie. I just came across your New York Student Council Conference in November. Looks awesome. I was just curious if you started reviewing speakers yet. Thanks, Grant." He wouldn't promote himself or send along a link to his speaker video: he'd just inquire. Often that would spark a dialogue or the recipient might proactively go check out his site.

At a minimum, the recipient would answer his question and tell him they planned to start looking at speakers in a few weeks or a few months. He'd make a note in his calendar and follow up—a step that shockingly few people take. But that gave him a critical advantage. "If someone's planning a state conference and it happens once a year, there's a very small window out of 365 days where they're going to be looking to hire a speaker," he says. "If you're outside of that window on either side, then you miss it until next year. It's just trying to catch them at the right time." By creating a small, positive initial interaction—and then showcasing his diligence and reliability by following up—Baldwin set himself apart.

His response-rate percentages still weren't great. "If you sent a hundred emails to people, you might hear back from five of them, and of those five, you may book one or two," he says. But those were two gigs he wouldn't have gotten otherwise, and they provided a critical early boost to his speaking career. As a result, he's been able to raise his fees and now has the luxury of scaling back his frenetic efforts. "Two years ago, I did sixty-seven events, and last year, I did twenty-nine events," he told me. "This year, I'll probably do ten . . . I'm married, I've got three little girls, so I just want to be home more." When you've built a solid foundation, you have the flexibility to make choices like that.

Try This:

As you're considering inbound and outbound marketing strategies, ask yourself:

- What techniques will you use to get conference organizers to come to you (blogging, appearing on podcasts, referrals from colleagues, etc.)? Make a list of at least two specific tactics you plan to implement in the next three months.

- Identify your targets. Create a list of at least five conferences where you'd like to speak. Look up the program chair's contact information online and, in the next week, send a short email inquiry to each of them. Repeat on a weekly basis.

Expand Your Network and Monetize in Other Ways

One of the biggest challenges in the speaking world is the fact that, even if you've done an incredible job, you likely won't be hired again, at least for several years, because there's a constant quest for "fresh perspectives" and "new blood."

That's why one of the best steps you can take is building relationships with other speakers who can provide you with valuable information about the going rate at various conferences and can recommend you to decision makers. My friend Mike Michalowicz, author of *Profit First* and *Surge*, created a speaker-referral group that he invited me to join. As a result of the connections I made, I landed paid gigs in Puerto Rico and Slovakia, and I also referred opportunities to several other members.

In addition to going wider and getting more business through referrals, you can also go deeper and earn more revenue for each engagement by thinking creatively. In the early days of his speaking business, Baldwin would offer a day rate of $1,500, and would often do two to three talks that day to different groups of attendees. Since he was already on site, he figured it wouldn't be too much additional effort to do a second or third talk. He also knew it would help his referral stream if he could get in front of more potential customers. And, critically, the arrangement allowed him to charge more than the $500 or $1,000 he would have normally gotten at the time for just one speech.

Baldwin is also a fan of identifying alternate revenue sources tied to the speaking engagement (with the organizer's permission, of course). This is especially beneficial if you're speaking for free or a reduced price. For instance, he self-published a book that he alludes to in his talk and is frequently able to sell at the back of the room afterward. "We've sold over thirty thousand physical copies of the book, and 95 percent of that has come as a direct result of speaking," he says.

Similarly, speaker Chris Widener told me in an interview for *Forbes* that when he's speaking for free at certain conferences, he'll create a one-page order form for his various products, such as DVDs and books, and ask the organizers to place a copy on everyone's seat.[2] "With about ten minutes left in the speech, I'll say, 'I want to let you know about some great materials; all you have to do is fill out this form and turn it in to me at the end. We'll ship it to you in a week.'" He says that 20 to 35 percent of the audience typically makes a purchase. "I've spoken to three thousand people and sold $140,000 in product after a speech." Of course, making a pitch and selling products at the back of the room generally isn't accepted if you're speaking to a corporate audience; you need to understand what's appropriate in that venue. But it's always useful to at least think about nontraditional possibilities for monetizing around your talks.

That's because speaking—while it's a great way to earn a living for those who enjoy it—isn't always the most reliable or predictable source of income. During recessions especially, companies almost always scale back on conferences and the speakers who populate them. And the work is very seasonal; I travel almost nonstop during the spring and fall "high season" for conferences, and business slows down dramatically in the summer and over the holiday season. Additionally, because there's a glut of free competition, it can be a long, slow process to separate yourself from the competition and build your brand (witness the fact that it took Schawbel three years of speaking for free to land his first paid speech).

Finally, because of the long lead time in planning conferences, even once you start gaining momentum with your speaking practice, you can't abandon other revenue sources. "If I book something right now that happens in nine months, that's awesome in nine months, but I still have bills to pay today," says Baldwin. "It takes a while to build up enough on your calendar to even out the cash flow cycles where it works out for you." As he was building his nascent speaking business, he worked as a restaurant waiter, a salesman for a security company, and more. As he developed his business and started to land more gigs, he was able to slowly quit his part-time jobs.

Once you've begun to build your speaking business, it's essential to grow your audience and bring in more leads. Podcasting, the topic of the next chapter, is one of the best ways to do just that.

Try This:

If you're just starting your speaking career, focus on booking gigs first. But it doesn't hurt to start to think about alternative income streams for the future. Ask yourself:

- What products, such as books or audio learning kits, could you create? What aspects of your talk most interest your audience, and where could they benefit by going deeper?

- Start to do preliminary research. If you were going to self-publish a workbook or create a video training course, what resources (including time, money, and equipment) would you need to accomplish that? Ask colleagues and look for reference articles online. It's useful to understand what might be possible in the future, so you can start taking initial steps, such as recording talks for later use in training modules.

CHAPTER 6

Build a Following through Podcasting

When podcasting was invented in 2004, it wasn't an immediate sensation. Jason Van Orden recalls the first time he heard the term: "I Googled it, and Google came back with, 'Did you mean . . . ?' It tried to correct me. Google didn't know what podcasting was, either."

But Van Orden, who had some programming skills, was interested enough to keep digging. "I eventually found a few geek blog posts, talking about MP3 closures and the RSS 2.0 spec or something." The vibe, he says, was "guys who had just found their dad's ham radio in a garage."

Fortunately, things have become much simpler for people interested in building a following through podcasting. Just as website creation has become democratized (you don't need to know HTML in order to set up a WordPress site these days), podcasting has also gone from an arcane, technically complex endeavor to a popular pursuit. As of June 2015, there were more than two hundred thousand unique podcasts listed in Apple's iTunes directory.[1] Even more are expected to come online in the next few years, as analysts estimate that by 2025, all new cars will be connected to the internet.[2]

When that day comes, "radio" and "podcasts" will be virtually interchangeable, and that makes podcasting extremely desirable for big business. As Jordan Harbinger, the host of the popular *Art of Charm* podcast, predicts, "That Top 100 [iTunes] real estate is going to be all corporations that spend millions of dollars marketing their shows. There'll be 80 Discovery Channel podcasts, 100 ESPN podcasts, and to be in the Top 100 is going to be damn near impossible."[3] But right now, he believes—even if it seems as if everyone already has a podcast and the competition is impossible—there's still a moment to sneak in and make your mark.

As you think about using podcasting to monetize your own future, consider the following topics: focusing on frequency and longevity; attracting advertising revenue; and generating business leads.

Focus on Frequency and Longevity

When Harbinger and his partner started their own podcast more than a decade ago, at first he was rather haphazard about the process, recording episodes intermittently and not focusing on listener data. "One day, we saw we had twenty-four downloads. Not twenty-four thousand, and not twenty-four hundred. We had twenty-four . . . We didn't check our stats again, probably, for six years. It didn't really start as a business. It was just kind of this fun thing that we do."

But around 2012, he decided to increase the frequency with which he published episodes. He started "releasing every single week on the same day, at the same time, and my audience kind of doubled overnight." So he kept it up, releasing twice a week, and his downloads once again more than doubled. He finally settled on releasing three episodes per week, and now draws more than three million downloads per month.

As Harbinger's experience shows, frequency is key to podcasting success. Another, quite simply, is longevity. Podcasts need time to build up a listenership, and many podcasters quit in the interim because they conclude their efforts aren't working. But as some of the most successful podcasters have discovered, there's a disproportionate reward for sticking around long enough to break through.

A detailed analysis by Josh Morgan showed that "between June 2005 and June 2015, a typical podcast ran for six months and twelve episodes, at two episodes per month, before going inactive."[4] According to his research, only 40 percent of the 206,000 podcasts were "active" between January and June 2015, which he defined, quite liberally, as publishing only one new episode during that time period. It's no wonder the vast majority of podcasters aren't building a following if they give up so quickly. There may be a huge number of podcasts, but competition is a lot easier to manage when you realize that most people don't stay in the game very long.

I'm no exception. I flirted with the idea of creating a podcast back in 2009 and interviewed a few friends for it. Mostly, for a while, I uploaded audio clips from speeches that I gave. But I never managed to settle on a regular publishing schedule; I once waited eleven months between uploads and finally deleted the account when I realized I hadn't added anything new in more than two years.

The benefits of podcasting—when you apply yourself diligently, as I have *not* done—are substantial. But there's also an opportunity cost. If you're creating episodes multiple times a week, there are plenty of other things you can't do. I've chosen, instead, to focus on writing books and blogging as my primary forms of content creation (as well as being a guest on other people's podcasts, including more than 160 of them in 2015 alone, as I launched my previous book, *Stand Out*).

In order to be successful, you have to prioritize, and I didn't pick podcasting. But *if you can commit* to keeping up the discipline and can grow your audience, it's a great way to build a brand and monetize. Below, we'll look at how to do so through advertising revenues.

Try This:

As you're plotting what kind of podcast you might create, do the following:

- Go on iTunes and download episodes from at least ten podcasts in your field. Listen to all of them over the course of the next couple of weeks and identify what elements you like most and least. How will yours be different and unique?

- What subject-matter niche would you like your podcast to fill? (It's hard to gain traction with a topic as broad as "sports" or "marketing.")

- What style would you like your podcast to be in? Friendly? Authoritative? Will you have a cohost?

Attract Advertising Revenue

John Lee Dumas attributes his success with his award-winning *Entrepreneur on Fire* podcast to his laserlike focus. He describes his early mentality: "I am going to generate revenue [through] podcasting; this is my focus; this is what I'm going to do 100 percent . . . That's why I quit my job, I had a mentor, I went all in."

You don't necessarily need to quit your job to start a podcast—that's almost always inadvisable—but Dumas's commitment was essential to his success. That's because, he recalls, "For the first nine months—three months prelaunch and then six months postlaunch—there was no revenue. Every month, we were going a little further in the red."

That's a typical experience for many first-time podcasters. Advertisers aren't interested in most fledgling podcasts, which often draw only a few hundred listeners. But once you reach a certain threshold—Harbinger estimates it at ten thousand downloads per episode—your show begins to look like a smart way to reach a sophisticated audience (because, while growing in popularity, podcasts still aren't mainstream and are disproportionately listened to by younger, tech-savvy consumers). Pat Flynn, for instance, receives between eighty thousand and a hundred thousand downloads per episode of *Smart Passive Income*. As a result, he says, "Generally speaking, for each sponsor that I have on the show, it's between $2,500 and $4,000, so it's quite a substantial amount of money per episode."

Advertising rates are calculated on the basis of each one thousand downloads; that figure is known as the cost per mille (CPM). Rates change frequently and aren't set in stone. But as of the time of this writing, the CPM was significantly higher for podcasts than for traditional radio. This is likely because listeners have to consciously subscribe to and download episodes of podcasts, showing their engagement with the material, while radio listeners may be listening more passively or have accidentally flipped to a station.

Harbinger estimates that a typical advertising rate for podcasts might be $20 CPM, those with "premium audiences" that are particularly desirable to advertisers can draw $30 to $35 CPM, and those with "super niche" audiences—people who would be very hard to reach through other advertising channels—could earn as much as $100 CPM. A 2016 *Wall Street Journal* article concurred that top podcasts can receive a CPM of $50–$100.[5]

Podcasts are also far more lucrative for their creators on a per-listener basis than YouTube videos. Says Harbinger, "Somebody who's got millions of YouTube views, they'll make less than somebody who's got thousands or tens of thousands of podcast downloads." Estimates vary regarding YouTube's CPM, and some place it as high as $18, but some YouTubers are receiving far less.[6] They're not supposed to disclose exact numbers, but in a 2015 *Medium* post, popular video blogger Hank Green reported receiving a mere $2 CPM.[7]

Advertising isn't the only way to make money through podcasting, of course. Harbinger sells slots for his in-person *Art of Charm* trainings; Pat Flynn earns tens of thousands of dollars per month in affiliate deals; and John Lee Dumas has created a robust membership community called Podcasters' Paradise.

We'll discuss all of these strategies in more depth in subsequent chapters, but for now, let's look at one old-fashioned strategy for monetizing podcasts: using them as a business development tool.

Try This:

If you think a podcast might be a good fit for you, consider taking the following actions:

- Make a list of ten "shoo-in" guests that you could have on your initial episodes as you get the hang of the medium. You don't want to start out by approaching world-famous people you don't know well. Instead, focus on people in the field you'd like to target for your podcast, but with whom you already have a good relationship. That way, they'll be more likely to say yes to you and more tolerant of any rookie mistakes you might make.

- Schedule your first interviews and launch with at least three episodes at once (if not more). That shows that you're serious and also juices your initial download numbers, so you're more likely to gain traction on iTunes.

Generate Business Leads

Fei Wu was a digital producer and web developer at a Boston-based advertising agency. She started her podcast, *Feisworld*, in October 2014 in order to connect with people she admired, such as business leaders and creative professionals. She was persistent—she released about an episode per week for her first eighteen months—but her listenership was very slow to build. "It's somewhere in the fifteen thousand to twenty thousand download range," she told me. Per episode? Per month? No, total.

It was a far cry from the ten thousand downloads *per show* that Harbinger indicated was the minimum threshold to pique advertisers' interest. Yet, thanks in large part to her podcast, Wu was able to quit her day job and launch her own full-time freelance business.

Of the nearly forty guests who have appeared on her show at the time of this writing, close to 25 percent have become clients of her consulting business—an astonishing conversion rate, especially since podcasting was never a conscious lead-generation strategy for her.

It started in July 2015, when she received Cirque du Soleil tickets for her birthday. She was immediately struck by the mastery of two performers, the brothers Kevin and Andy Atherton, whom she describes as "superhuman." She wanted them on her podcast.

She went to their website to find their email address and found herself . . . confused. It wasn't clear how to contact them, and she recalls, "I noticed on their website that the top navigation [bar] was about ten to twelve items . . . there was a lot of overlapping information." She finally located their email address, had them on the show, and the interview was great.

But a few weeks later, she still couldn't get their unwieldy website out of her head. As a digital professional, she knew they could do so much better. She wanted to say something, but she hesitated. "I wasn't sure who designed the original website, and I was afraid to have people's feelings hurt," she recalls. She finally decided to send a gently worded email, praising them for having a website in the first place, but suggesting that with a new show on the horizon, this was an opportunity for a refresh.

She didn't pitch herself; instead, she laid out a series of suggestions, ranging from reorganizing their content to sharing behind-the-scenes videos. "I even created a Google Doc for them, so they could remember and refer back to it," she said.

They wrote back right away, she recalls. They agreed with her suggestions, but didn't know how to implement them. "How would you go about it?" they asked her. "What's your rate?"

They weren't the only podcast guests who later became clients. Kristina Reed was an Academy Award–winning film producer who had made her mark on such films as *Kung Fu Panda*, *Madagascar*, and *Shrek the Third*, but was starting to think about her next chapter. She knew that Wu was also considering a leap into working for herself. Ten months after their interview, Wu recalls, "She said, 'Fei, do you have half an hour? I really want to catch up with you.'" After years of working inside Hollywood studios, Reed didn't have her own online presence and hired Wu to help.

Wu has also had podcast guests request her help with marketing and PR projects. "I started doing [*Feisworld*] without any expectation of 'I need to make money,' or 'I need to eventually work for these people.' None of that." But by making genuine connections with her guests, they became curious about who she was and eventually realized they could benefit from her help.

Try This:

You're further along now and ready to take your podcast to the next level. It's time to consider the following actions:

- Now make a list of your top twenty *ideal* guests. Who are they (entrepreneurs, fitness experts, top architects)? Look them up online and find their contact information. In many cases, they'll have their own website with contact forms or email addresses provided; in other cases, you may only be able to locate their social media profiles. Make a spreadsheet.

- For each potential guest, think about the connections you have to them. If you know the individual personally, that's great. If not, could a mutual friend introduce you? Have they already been a guest on the podcast of someone you know? Ask them if they'd be willing to connect you. You'll be surprised at how many people will say yes.

CHAPTER 7

Develop Your Audience by Blogging and Vlogging

No matter where you are on your entrepreneurial path, creating a blog or video blog ("vlog") to develop your following may be a smart idea. Perhaps you're just starting out, and crafting a highly visible, profitable blog *is* your dream—an end in itself. Or maybe you see blogging as just one piece of a larger plan that includes a book rollout, coaching business, and live events. Either way, at some point, blogging or vlogging will likely be part of your journey to monetize.

It was for Stefanie O'Connell. Like many twenty-some-things with a dream, O'Connell moved to New York to become a Broadway actress. She would land a gig here or there, but soon discovered it wasn't enough to cover the city's exorbitant living expenses. That's when she started a blog, *The Broke and*

Beautiful Life, to keep herself on track and share with others the money tips she'd learned.

She began writing two or three times a week and enjoyed the process. Maybe, she realized, she could make ends meet by helping others learn to do the same. For months, she was writing on her own site and earning nothing. But as she gained experience, she realized she could "ladder up" and connect with slightly more experienced bloggers. "It wasn't high-level bloggers—not people with massive audiences," she recalls. But they could pay her $20 or $30 per article, so she started contributing to their blogs and building a reputation among their followers.

The money wasn't much, considering the effort she put in. But, she notes, "I had been an actress up until that time. For me, anything that was even twenty bucks, that was an hour I didn't have to wait tables." Her writing for other sites also served another valuable purpose: networking. "Beyond the fact that I made some money, I also established a presence such that I became a part of the personal finance community. People knew who I was," she said. That exposure proved to be a crucial step in her journey to becoming a recognized personal finance expert.

In this chapter, we'll explore lessons learned by bloggers like O'Connell and others as they discovered how to leverage the medium to build their reputation and bring in revenue. We'll talk about the importance of focusing on small wins; seeking out corporate sponsorship; starting and leveraging your own blog; and launching and monetizing a video blog.

Focus on Small Wins

As O'Connell discovered during her time writing $20 articles, working so hard for little money can become discouraging over time. But she kept herself motivated by focusing on each small success. She recalls the first time she was asked to sponsor a give-away on her site, which she considered important recognition because it was "somebody saying there's value here." Every time a more prominent blogger shared her work, or someone asked her to be a guest on their podcast, she celebrated. "They were little wins, but to me, they were huge," she says.

Writing for other bloggers' sites was a step up, but she knew she couldn't stop there. She had to establish herself as an expert by breaking through to larger, well-known publications. She began sending cold emails to prominent outlets, offering her-self as a potential contributor. "I usually didn't hear anything back." But finally, she did. She landed a column in *U.S. News & World Report*, and that gave her a higher profile. That, in turn, made her a desirable freelance contributor for startups looking to create their own content. It wasn't that much—often as little as $100 per post—but O'Connell had found a way to quintuple her income.

With a full panoply of clips and a prominent outlet behind her, O'Connell felt she could now present herself as a millennial finance expert. So she continued pitching, this time to television producers, suggesting ideas for potential topics she could speak about. Before long, *The Dr. Oz Show* and Fox News had both invited her to appear.

Building a reputation through blogging doesn't happen over-night; the path from your first post to national television appear-ances often takes years, and many give up before then. But in order to persevere, it's critical to take pleasure in the little victo-ries along the way, as O'Connell did, and recognize that even if you haven't arrived at your destination, you're still making prog-ress. It took me two to three years of blogging multiple times per week in order to start getting a meaningful number of inbound inquiries, such as requests for interviews or speeches.

Even once you get there, an expert reputation and television appearances are fantastic forms of social proof, but by themselves, they still don't pay the bills. You can't write enough $100 articles per week to live comfortably in New York City. But even as it gets harder to make money *by* writing, it becomes easier to make money *because of* your writing—in the form of corporate sponsorships.

Try This:

To create your blogging wish list, start here:

- Make a list of publications you'd like to write for. Think big—national outlets—but also small. Where could you start out? Are there local publications or smaller niche sites in your field? Start to map out a ladder strategy in which you'll plan to write for lower-profile outlets and steadily work your way up. For instance, when I was starting my consulting business in Boston years ago, I began by writing for my own blog, so I had some sample material to show editors (you could also do this on LinkedIn or *Medium*). Then, I began reaching out to venues like my local paper (the *Somerville Journal*) and the local business paper (the *Boston Business Journal*). You could also target industry-specific blogs, newspapers, or magazines, or your regional daily (such as the *Boston Globe* or *San Francisco Chronicle*). Finally, when you feel ready, you can reach out to household-name publications that utilize outside contributors, such as (in the business world) *Forbes* or *Inc.* or *Business Insider*. By then, you'll have a solid array of clips and will have enough experience to be taken seriously when the editors evaluate your materials.

Seek Out Corporate Sponsorship

As a blogger, O'Connell gets invited to a lot of conferences and events sponsored by corporations. But unlike most people who sit back and enjoy the speakers and the canapés, she meticulously records how the event is structured, so she can propose her own variation to the sponsors. She says, "Clearly, the company's already decided this is a worthwhile investment for them. I don't have to convince them of that . . . How do I give new value, such that I'm incorporating myself into it in a way that is indispensable?" In other words, she's looking for low-hanging fruit.

Because she's already developed a relationship with the company, often through the PR people who invited her to attend, she has a contact she can pitch ideas to. As one example, she attended a "Women in Money Tea" and brainstormed a millennial twist: What if it were a bar trivia night focused on personal finances? She pitched the idea to another company that held similar events, and it agreed.

Pricing your involvement in corporate events is an inexact science, as payment terms are usually private and opaque. "My greatest strategy is asking people who have done it before," O'Connell says. "That's the only way I can get a frame of reference for what's appropriate." The variation is enormous, and companies are often able to pay far more than they initially claim. She was once offered $500 for an engagement, which she ultimately negotiated up to $5,000. "That's why I'm always telling people to think bigger," she says. "There's so much opportunity out there. They have the budgets for this, and we're offering value."

Another time, she earned $8,000 to blog about a study that a company had commissioned and then create a video about the findings and share it widely on social media. Once you build your brand to the point where you're considered a recognized expert, companies—if pushed just hard enough—are often willing and able to pay.

Unless you become a household-name celebrity (as opposed to a niche expert), it's unlikely that you can support yourself on corporate sponsorships alone. But if you cultivate and nurture the connections, they can represent a very healthy complement to your income. That's been the case of Alexandra Levit, the author of *They Don't Teach Corporate in College.* "I've never made, on an individual sponsorship gig, more than . . . $25,000 a year." But she often has multiple corporate engagements at one time and other streams of income from writing, speaking, and consulting. "So I'm piecing together a living that's very, very good for an individual," she says.

She's served as a spokesperson for numerous *Fortune* 500 brands, which hire her to create content that's relevant to their audience and speak about it through various media opportunities. "I'm not going to hawk their product," she says. "I'm going to talk about what I always talk about, which is productivity, how to be an entrepreneur, and how to engage a successful strategy to grow your business."

Like O'Connell, Levit typically lands the sponsorship gigs through PR professionals who come across her work. What the company is looking for, she says, is someone who has a strong platform that can spread its message. "You have to have some sort of a public persona," she says. "Then these assignments feed other assignments, because you get one and then Canon will see what you did with Xerox."

The process of landing corporate sponsorships can be very slow, however. "There might not be an immediate payoff," says Levit. "It's kind of like any other form of networking, where you're just getting to know people, and you learn more about what they do and figure out ways that you could potentially help them."

While she doesn't write about her existing clients, she'll often get pitched by PR people she doesn't know, hoping to win coverage for their clients. She considers that a relationship-building opportunity: "If there's a way I can work in their angle or something they're doing, I'm going to do it. I'm not going to say, 'You have to pay me $500 for that.' If it works for me and it works for them, then I'm going to respond to them."

She's also willing to accept small gigs at first, to prove herself and deepen the connection. A while back, a PR firm asked her to participate in a Twitter chat hosted by Bank of America. "It wasn't very much money at all, but I looked at it as a chance to meet Bank of America folks," she says. "I didn't know if this would result in something significant, but it was a way to start with them . . . You have to be willing to give a little before you can get. I think that's networking and that's part of life." When it comes to corporate sponsorship opportunities, you have to play the long game.

Try This:

As you explore sponsorships, keep in mind the following:

- Start to keep a log of the publicists who may be contacting you: Who do they represent? And based on media reports or events you've been invited to, take note of which brands in your field are sponsoring which type of events. Would you be interested in working with their company? What analogous events or offerings could you propose?

Start Your Own Blog

O'Connell built her reputation through blogging relentlessly on other sites, working her way up to well-known outlets like *U.S. News & World Report*, which provided her with the social proof to attract corporate sponsors. Levit did much the same through writing five books, and, for a time, writing regularly for the *Wall Street Journal*. But there's also another brand-building possibility: starting your own blog and developing an organic following. That's what Minnesota resident Bjork Ostrom and his wife Lindsay did.

Lindsay loved cooking and, Bjork recalls, "she was starting to share recipes on Facebook and Twitter with her personal network. It got to the point where she's like, 'I wonder if I'm doing this a little bit too much, and maybe they're getting a little bit annoyed.'" So, in April 2010, they decided to launch a blog together called *Pinch of Yum*. Lindsay, a teacher, handled the creative aspects—developing recipes, writing, and food photography. Bjork, who was working in the programs division of a nonprofit but had a side interest in websites and business development, handled the technical side.

Growth wasn't exactly explosive. But like O'Connell, they focused on the small victories. "I think for Lindsay, it was the game of it," Bjork says. "It's like, *How do I get a comment on a post? How do you get to a hundred visitors a day?* It's these micro-goals along the way." After two years of creating regular content, they were only at a thousand unique visitors per day. But, around then, their persistence began to pay off: they were starting to rank near the top of search engine results and had created recipes for a wide variety of meals; through Google and Pinterest, people were beginning to discover them.

"In your first year or two, you're in the building stages, and you're really trying to ramp up the [user] engagement and the attention your site is getting," says Bjork. "It has the potential to be distracting if you focus too much on creating an income in the early stages before really ramping things up." In other words, content first, monetization afterward.

Leverage Your Growing Audience

By 2016, six years after starting their blog, the Ostroms began reaching nearly 3 million unique visitors per month. That's a lot of eyeballs, and on a recent visit to their site, the sidebar featured ads from the *New York Times*, Staples, and Hotels.com. But Bjork cautions against focusing on display ads as your primary monetization strategy: "The thing with display advertising is that as the effectiveness of it goes down [due to consumer overload], so does the earning potential with it. Long term, it's probably not the best strategy to build off of."

It's also not particularly accessible to most nascent online entrepreneurs. You'll likely need to have more than a hundred thousand monthly unique visitors in order to be considered of interest to display advertisers, notes Bjork; even then, the rates are modest, maybe $500 per month for a food blog with that level of readership. Blogs on certain other topics, such as personal finance, are slightly more lucrative. "It depends on the niche that you're in," he says. "It's not like people are buying a ton of food stuff online now." But overall, display advertising isn't where you're going to make most of your money.

As with O'Connell and Levit, part of the Ostroms' revenue model comes from corporate sponsorships—in their case, sponsored posts. For instance, Lindsay would create a recipe and blog post featuring a certain brand of sugar and disclose that sponsorship at the top. Yet another revenue stream comes from affiliate income. Like Pat Flynn of *Smart Passive Income*, they earn thousands of dollars a month in referral fees. For instance, they've created an exhaustive post on "How to Start a Food Blog." Step one recommends securing a domain name and setting up your website. They explain in detail how to do this and receive a referral fee from the hosting service they recommend for every sign-up.

For the uninitiated, "making money from your blog" might sound like one simple revenue stream. But as the Ostroms show, once you've built an audience, you can monetize that one resource in myriad ways. In addition to display ads, sponsored posts, and affiliate income, Lindsay has written a popular ebook on food photography, and they've started to offer workshops on the subject, which have earned them tens of thousands of dollars.

Like Flynn and Dumas, Bjork was committed to sharing what he learned about online marketing, so he began posting monthly income reports in September 2011, a year and a half after the blog launched. That month, the Ostroms earned $21.97 from advertising on their site. But just over five years later, their monthly tally looked rather different: over $95,000 during November 2016 alone, which is more than most teachers or nonprofit staffers make in an entire year. "A few steps, taken every day, really add up over a long period of time," says Bjork.[1]

Try This:

- If you're blogging on your own site, think about ways to monetize it. For example: Which forms of monetization might work for you? Display ads? Sponsored posts?

Affiliate income? Selling ebooks? Pick at least one to start with.

- Get specific about the monetization channel or channels you selected.

  - For instance, do you want display ads on your site, or do you feel it detracts from the overall reader experience? If you do want them, start looking into how you can sign up for Google's advertising program or other advertising networks.

  - Do some research on other sites to see which companies in your space already pay for sponsored posts; perhaps they'd be good targets to approach if your monthly page views are sufficient.

  - You can start to think about which products (that you believe in) would be good to promote as an affiliate. Is there content you can create that would highlight the product's virtues and link to a site where people can buy it?

  - What topics would appeal to your readers in ebook form? Is there something you do that's technical, or otherwise fairly involved, that is simply too complex to explain in a regular blog post? If so, perhaps an ebook might be the right format.

Launch Your Video Blog

The first text-based blog was created in 1994, but for more than a decade, sluggish internet speeds and the huge expense of recording equipment didn't permit most people to create and share videos without a lot of hassle.[2] But thanks to YouTube's creation in 2006, the increasing ubiquity of broadband, and the ease of recording with smartphones, anyone can now share their ideas and content in video format.

That was Antonio Centeno's plan when he was looking for ways to promote his online custom-clothing company. Drawn by the business opportunity, he says, "I started a clothier, but I didn't know anything about style." He read every book he could find, assimilated it, and started writing his own blog posts about men's fashion. But he soon realized he could reach even more potential customers if he took that content and repurposed it into video format.

"I started filming these videos in the basement of my house," he says. "The first one hundred videos honestly suck, but I learned a lot and got them out there." As with Bjork and Lindsay Ostrom, he realized that persistence was key. "After two hundred videos, we got to our first million views."

Centeno still regrets easing up his pace at that critical moment: "I was putting out one video a day for about 200 days. Then I slowed down after about 220 or 230. I was putting out only two a month. I always kick myself, because had I been more consistent, my channel would probably be twice the size it is now."

Indeed, well-known life coach Marie Forleo, mentioned in chapter 2, credits the rise of her eight-figure business in large part to her consistent video-blogging schedule. "Before MarieTV, I didn't have a regular blogging or newsletter schedule," she told *Forbes* in 2013.[3] "While I rarely went more than 10 days without communicating to my audience, everything changed when I committed to my Tuesday show. It's been 2.5 years of consistent content each week and that consistency has radically grown our online community."

As for Centeno, recognizing the promotional possibilities of his video blogging led him to question the business model of selling custom clothing. He says, "We were growing up, we were doing a very healthy six figures, and I realized, 'Wow, I'm going to lose money this year and I can't scale.'" Why couldn't he focus his business on the part that was working—providing fashion information?

Monetize Your Vlog

Centeno's first forays into marketing on his vlog felt like a burden. He would receive product samples from a company and then the clock would start ticking for him to write the review. The problem was he still had a full-time job, running his custom-clothing company. He recalls one company that sent him a pair of shoes, hoping for some publicity: "They kept emailing me every month like, 'Hey Antonio, how's that review coming?' I felt so bad because they had given me these free shoes and I just hadn't put out anything."

He realized two important things. First, he didn't want to do product reviews in exchange for free merchandise. "There's always a cost," he says. "The cost is not spending time with my family because I'm busy talking about these free shoes." Second, he had a big enough platform that he could start charging for access. He decided to shut down the custom-clothing business and go all-in on information marketing, especially leveraging his *Real Men, Real Style* YouTube channel, which, as of April 2017, had nearly 1.3 million subscribers and videos that have been viewed close to 94 million times.

Today, Centeno estimates that 25 to 30 percent of his revenue comes from advertising, especially sponsored articles and reviews. He says, "They realize we have a sizable, very specific audience, and they're going to pay me $5,000 for an article or they'll pay me $10,000 for a video article, plus email blast with social media promotion." His goal, he says, is that despite his full disclosure of the sponsorship, it "actually doesn't even feel like a commercial . . . 95 percent of it is solid information."

As an example, he cites a comprehensive article and video he created for his website called the "Ultimate Guide to Double Monk Strap Dress Shoes." At the top, he leads with a disclosure: "This informative article is brought to you by [shoe company] Paul Evans." Centeno writes, "I personally own a pair and highly recommend their quality shoes." He follows with a detailed history of the shoe style, color choices, and advice on pairing them with suits and casual attire, such as this pro tip: "A white V-neck t-shirt, blazer and blue jeans combination work well with a pair of brown suede double monk straps," writes Centeno.[4]

Like the Ostroms, Centeno also makes some money through the Amazon affiliate program and selling ebooks. He even offers a more in-depth course on men's fashion that costs thousands of dollars. But perhaps his most innovative move was teaming up with several other men's fashion bloggers to form MENfluential, an advertising network. They've hired a staffer to pitch their consortium as a group to menswear companies. Their combined reach makes them attractive to advertisers, and if Centeno's rates are too high, for instance, they can suggest another member of the group with a slightly smaller audience. The arrangement, says Centeno, "made Christmas very easy. We were booked for three months solid starting in mid-October."

His reach on YouTube is enormous, but Centeno recognizes the fragility of his fan base: "With social media, I don't own any of those platforms. I always realize even YouTube could shut me down. My goal is always to get people off of there, and onto my email list." He's created a popular free ebook, 7 Deadly Style Sins, that has gained him more than 100,000 daily email subscribers and allowed him to communicate directly with his audience.

But despite his wariness about YouTube as a platform, he remains clear on the power of video. "I find that video creates sales," he says. "They can tell I'm genuine, I'm real. Where I get the deepest connection is definitely through video."

Try This:

As you consider whether vlogging is right for you, try the following:

- Make a list of at least five other video bloggers (aka "vloggers") who focus on your space. Watch at least three to four of their most popular videos to get a feel for their style, approach, and what works. Decide what elements you want to emulate and what you'd like to do differently.

- If you decide you're interested in creating your own videos, write up an editorial calendar with at least twenty entries (i.e., a list of topics you'll be covering in future videos). Consistency is key; you'll need to produce content regularly to build up a following and gain the experience you need to excel.

- Think through how to make your videos stand out. It's not terrible to be a "talking head" explaining the same points that you would in a blog post, but it's even better if you can also express your points visually by doing a demonstration, showing an object, or using graphics to emphasize your point.

Video Tools

If you'd like to download a free list of the low-cost tools I use to make my own videos, you can access it at dorieclark.com/ videotools.

CHAPTER 8

Bring Your Followers Together

There's a special form of learning and connection that can only take place in a group environment. Once you've started to build a following—attracting interest through your speaking engagements, podcasts, or blogs, and working individually with coaching or consulting clients—you can start to bring them together in person.

The events can be large or small, and high ticket or low dollar. It's important to build your following first, because you can destroy your ROI quickly if you spend huge amounts of time hunting down participants to fill seats for an event. However, if you know you have a large enough audience, or even a small group that's highly engaged, in-person gatherings can be a remarkably effective way to earn revenue and provide your community with a unique and meaningful experience. Some ways to do this include creating a mastermind experience; organizing a conference; and offering in-person workshops. (We'll discuss how to create successful online communities later, in chapter 10.)

Create a Mastermind Experience

"Mastermind groups"—small groups of professionals who come together to share ideas and business advice—were first popularized in Napoleon Hill's classic *Think and Grow Rich*. The book itself is a bit dated now, but the idea is timeless. Nothing sharpens your thinking like a small band of trusted colleagues who are willing to challenge you, hold you accountable, and support you through difficult times.

Some mastermind groups are organized by motivated professionals who know they'd benefit from the camaraderie and insight, and don't charge anything to the other participants. But it can be challenging to assemble, run, and maintain a thriving group over the long term, and that is why paid mastermind groups have become a successful business model.

Note that launching a mastermind group probably shouldn't be your first entrepreneurial activity. You need to have developed real subject-matter expertise, often borne of consulting or coaching, so you can lead the group with confidence. And in order to attract participants to such an intimate (and often pricey) gathering, it's important to have cultivated at least a preliminary following of interested people. But once you have those basics under way, the concept can be powerful.

For example, once I felt I had developed a robust community around my ideas, I decided to test the waters by organizing a one-off "Mastermind Day" to see if my audience would be interested in the experience. Participants would gather for a group dinner the night before and then spend the day at my home in New York City, sharing their business challenges and getting help from me and the rest of the group.

I started by sending out a note to the forty-six participants of an online pilot course I was running. I knew many of the members had expressed a desire to meet each other in person. I included an online poll to see who would be interested in a gathering, and when I had enough positive responses, I announced a date and sent another email asking people to commit. I charged $1,000 per person and received $8,000 in payments in forty-eight hours; I sent another six personal email messages and landed the final two participants. In all, I spent about an hour marketing a $10,000 event for which I would get to work from home for a day, with no travel time.

Like me, Ryan Levesque—a marketing consultant who helps online businesses identify leads through surveys and quizzes—created a small in-person pilot to test demand for his eventual mastermind concept. "It was three of us organizing a group of maybe eight entrepreneurs," recalls Levesque, who is also the author of *Ask: The Counterintuitive Online Formula to Discover Exactly What Your Customers Want to Buy.* "We got in a room for two days, no curriculum, and it was just a hot seat

Mastermind Email

To download a copy of the email I sent out about my first Mastermind Day, visit dorieclark.com/MastermindEmail.

[in which people discussed the most pressing issue they faced]. People would come in, they'd get an hour to focus on their business . . . There was no structure . . . no thought to all the little things."

But this ad hoc event showed Levesque there was demand for a more intensive and planned-out experience. As a result, he decided to launch a mastermind group limited to forty participants. The group meets three times per year in Austin, Texas (where Levesque lives), for three days at a time. In between, they do weekly check-in calls and participate in an online community to share questions, successes, and struggles.

The in-person sessions are meant to transport participants out of their day-to-day lives, with healthy gourmet food, mornings spent discussing business issues, and afternoons and evenings on "experiential" activities meant to enhance bonding, from hatchet throwing to pub trivia to karaoke. The price tag? A hefty $35,000 per year; Levesque ultimately plans to raise it to $50,000, but is grandfathering early adopters to encourage sign-ups.

Running group programs is a great idea in theory: the leverage and earning potential are immense. But unlike a one-on-one coaching program, where you can extend the offer and not risk anything if no one signs up, group programs are trickier: you somehow need to establish demand early on for the program to succeed. How can you land those initial participants?

Levesque, whose business depends on teaching others how to survey customers, has thought this through. "Building a mastermind [group] that has two people in it . . . is not worth your time," he says. Instead, he describes how he initially approached his audience to gauge interest. He sent an email saying that he often gets asked about working with clients in a more intimate setting. Then, he laid out the vision for a possible mastermind group—meeting in person, three times a year, plus an online community and weekly call.

"There will only be 20 spots [initially] available for this," he wrote, "and if this is something you might be interested in if I decide to go forward, and you'd like to get a spot in line to be notified when it does become available, click on the link below. It's a simple link to make a $100 fully refundable deposit. If you change your mind, or if the mastermind group doesn't materialize, you can get it back. Meantime, this is a way for me to gauge who's seriously interested in this. If enough people are interested, then it's something I'll do."

With this strategy, Levesque hasn't definitively promised his followers anything; they won't feel offended or betrayed if he doesn't end up launching the mastermind group. By asking them to lay down some money—albeit a much smaller investment than the ultimate $35,000—he's able to determine who's reasonably serious about the proposition. And he can wait to launch until he has the magic number of participants, so the experience can be robust, as well as sufficiently remunerative for him. (For more detailed advice from other pros, see the sidebar "How to Start Your Own Paid Mastermind Group" at the end of this chapter.)

Try This:

If the idea of running a Mastermind Day appeals to you, ask yourself:

- Who would be most interested in attending (i.e., your target audience)? Would you do a series of hot seats, or focus on a specific theme? If so, which one? What would you charge for your pilot session? Write up a description (at least half a page and no more than one page in length).

• Write down the names of between ten and twenty specific people you know personally who match your target audience description. Send them a brief email and attach your Mastermind Day description. Ask if they'd be willing to offer feedback and whether they'd be interested in attending. If you keep hearing "no," modify your offering according to the suggestions you receive. If you hear a lot of yeses, schedule a date and start locking in commitments.

Organize a Conference

Levesque's mastermind groups are high-dollar, high-intensity experiences that last for a year or even more, if participants re-up. But you can also create short-term events for your followers that generate significant income. Social Media Marketing World—the conference where I spoke for free in order to have a chance to connect with so many of my speaker friends—charges between $850 and $1,600 for admission, depending on when you buy your ticket. In 2016, it drew three thousand attendees. When you're not paying for speakers, that's a *very* good rate of return.

The secret, according to conference founder Michael Stelzner, is that he started by knowing a lot of writers, based on connections from his previous company, which taught people how to get paid to write white papers (a topic of obvious interest to unemployed journalists). In the late 2000s, when he realized social media was becoming popular, he asked some of them if they'd be willing to contribute long-form articles to his new website, Social Media Examiner, for free.

The promise of exposure usually doesn't mean much, but in this case, it was true. There was a paucity of in-depth, knowledgeable articles about social media and a great deal of interest. Before long, his author friends were becoming widely recognized for their expertise, and Social Media Examiner had built a massive following: in 2015 alone, it added 250,000 subscribers. With those kind of numbers—when "exposure" actually means something—it's not hard to get volunteers to write or speak for free.

And like me, many speakers will at least sometimes sign on to events if it gives them a chance to reconnect with their friends or meet their heroes. That was the dynamic that fueled the unlikely success of Jayson Gaignard, the founder of Mastermind Talks, in the conference world.

It was August 2012, and Gaignard was in a bad place. He'd built a successful ticket-resale business in Canada, but—never a sports or live music fan—he hated the industry and wanted to get out. He'd also fallen $250,000 into debt, with a six-month-old baby and an impending wedding. Because of his daughter, he often kept unusual hours, which is why he was awake at 4 a.m. when Tim Ferriss's email came through.

Ferriss, author of *The 4-Hour Workweek,* was a business hero of Gaignard's. A few months later, Ferriss would release his much anticipated sequel, *The 4-Hour Chef.* But the book's success was at risk because Ferriss had inked a deal with Amazon to publish the book, and brick-and-mortar bookstores, such as Barnes & Noble, were refusing to stock it in protest. To juice sales, Ferriss needed to think creatively. So—a noted night owl—he sent a wee-hours missive to his email list, advertising a unique opportunity: if you preordered a whopping four thousand copies of his new book for a total of $84,000, he would give two keynote talks for you or your organization.

Despite the price tag, Gaignard knew the offer wouldn't last. "This is a great opportunity for anyone," he thought. So he immediately emailed Ferriss and accepted the deal. "I had basically two days, three days at most, to raise $84,000," he says. He had no idea how he would find the money, or even what he'd do with Ferriss's time, but he knew he'd figure it out. That day, he reached out to three friends who he thought might be able to help. The first one wanted to talk numbers and ROI; Gaignard simply didn't have the time. The second one was interested in something far more elaborate and wanted to launch a business together. But Gaignard could only focus on one thing: finding the money.

Finally, he called his third friend, who told him, "Come to my office tomorrow; you can pick up the bank draft." There was no contract, no nothing. Gaignard's network had come through for him, and with this new opportunity, he wondered if he could leverage the power of Ferriss's own network of friends and fans.

Gaignard knew that Ferriss was a cult figure in the business world—someone who even high-profile celebrities wanted in their orbits. He realized he could create a marquee event from scratch, using Ferriss as the linchpin. "I could get people who wanted to be connected with Tim to speak, or people who were already connected with Tim, but they were never at the same place at the same time," Gaignard recalls. "I could use the event as a catalyst to reconnect him with all his friends." As a result, he was able to land a powerhouse group of speakers for his event, including designer Marc Ecko and authors Ryan Holiday, James Altucher, and A. J. Jacobs.

Gaignard also created a small financial incentive, meant to spur competition—a $25,000 prize for the best talk. One speaker, he recalls, "actually had a $30,000 speaking gig that he turned down to come speak at Mastermind Talks to compete for the $25,000." He lost. But with Gaignard's clever strategy to help speakers build their own elite network, that speaker had clearly deemed it a worthwhile gamble.

Deciding What to Charge Attendees for Your Conference

The next question for Gaignard, of course, was what to charge attendees. Despite his experience reselling sports tickets, he initially wasn't sure what to charge. After all, he had never organized his own event.

He knew that the higher the price tag, the more exclusivity the event would project. And a premium ticket price would also give him more freedom to select attendees. But with no previous track record, he was hesitant to charge top dollar. What if no one was interested in signing up?

Several successful friends advised him that the maximum he could charge was $1,000 per ticket, but he decided to do an "A/B" test, in which he offered the same ticket at different prices as an experiment, to verify the assumption. It turns out his friends were wrong.

"I wanted to curate the audience, and the nice thing was, in raising the price point to $3,300, we had just as many people sign up—but they were better quality professionals," he says. In the end, Gaignard was able to draw 4,200 applications for $3,300 seats at his first event, all people lured by the chance to see Ferriss and other prominent speakers. He selected 150, vetting them with personal phone calls to ensure they'd add to the group dynamic. He says, "My philosophy is to do an experience with a small group, overdeliver, capture that experience on camera, and then you'll never have to sell the event ever again."

He's organized multiple Mastermind Talks conferences, but leaves open the possibility that he might stop at any time. "Once the event is done [for the year], I never commit to another one right away," he says. "I sit with it, and I just consider, *do I want to do this again?*" He doesn't want the events to get boring or repetitive—for him or for the audience.

"If you use the same venue and the same format, it's easy to compare, 'Oh, the first year was better than the second,'" Gaignard says. "But now that we're doing a traveling event, every venue is different, every format is different, and therefore every experience is different. It's a lot more work, because if I use the same venue as last year, I could plan that in a weekend . . . There's a great saying, 'Go the extra mile, because it's never crowded,' and this is one of the areas where a lot of people get sloppy."

In addition to changing the venue each year—from Toronto to California, and in between—Gaignard has also more than doubled the price, up to $7,500 for the 2016 gathering, nearly as much as the $8,500 price tag that the internationally renowned TED conference charged at the time. With the thousands of applicants the event drew from its inception, it would have been easy to throw open the doors and dramatically increase its size. But that would have spoiled what was most special about the event, Gaignard believes. "What makes Mastermind Talks unique is its intimacy," he says. "So instead of scaling in size, every year we raise the price point, and we raise the caliber of people in attendance."

Partly this is done through his meticulous personal interviews of new applicants. He describes refunding $48,000 in paid tickets—money that was already in his account—for prospective attendees of his first conference whom he deemed to be a poor fit. But Gaignard also takes the unusual step of culling prior attendees who are interested in returning. "We historically allow only one-third of attendees to come back," he says, in order to keep the conference fresh. For his 2015 conference in Napa, "we had 107 order forms for those 45 [returning] spots. Picking those 45 people was brutal."

Gaignard pays close attention at the event itself, "and there's a thousand reasons why I could decline somebody," he says. "If somebody's inauthentic and they project themselves a little differently than who they truly are, that's a reason. I had one person this year who was very, very successful, but wasn't coachable. He'd come to the event and act like a know-it-all." But sometimes, there just isn't enough room for everyone who wants to participate. He says, "This is the biggest pain point in this business; gearing up for those sixty uncomfortable conversations as to why people can't come back is tough."

In the end, however, Gaignard's model allows him to curate a highly lucrative event for which he's the sole gatekeeper. By enabling others to build better networks, he's succeeded in putting himself at the center of one of the business world's most elite.

Try This:

If you're interested in planning a conference, think about the following:

- Make a list of the best and worst conferences you've personally attended. What did you like most or least? Why? How could you create an event that reflects your own preferences and values? What would make your conference distinctive in the marketplace?

- If you're interested in organizing a conference, start mapping out the specifics of your future vision. Where would you hold it? What time of year? How large would it be? What speakers would you host? Would the conference have an overall theme? What would attendees get out of coming? How is that different from other conferences currently on the market?

- In a general sense—and well before committing to any course of action—start scoping out the pricing. It's useful to know more details so you can make an informed decision. What are conference center rental fees? How about food and drink? What does it take to reserve a block of rooms at the hotel? How far in advance do you need to book? What are cancellation policies? What is the keynote rate for the speakers you most want to land? A few phone calls can help you establish a ballpark estimate, and that allows you to determine whether and when you should launch.

Offer In-Person Workshops

Levesque runs ongoing mastermind groups, and Gaignard organizes a yearly conference with speakers and networking. But another model for monetizing in-person gatherings of your followers is to hold training and workshops.

Michael Port, the author of *Book Yourself Solid*, started his career as a New York University–trained professional actor. He excelled onstage, and speaking and presentations became a core part of his business. But for years, it never occurred to him that he could build a business around helping others do the same. Eventually, though, he received enough requests for coaching around public speaking that he took note.

He says, "So many of the people in the *Book Yourself Solid* community also did speaking engagements, either professionally or, for most of them, to spread their message and to book business from it. I said, 'Let me pilot it.'" At first, he began by offering a one-day master class on public speaking, and when it was well received, he expanded it to two days. He wanted to be sure there was really a market for it. "I probably did eight master classes over the course of a year and a half," he estimates.

Once he had established demand around public speaking training, he built a suite of offerings related to it. In 2015, he released a new book, *Steal the Show*, laying out his speaking methodology, which served as a driver of attention and leads. He also created a $500 online course around the concept of "Heroic Public Speaking," and held a large, annual gathering to bring participants together, with tickets ranging from $1,000 to $6,000, depending on the package selected. In its first year, Port invited me to present on a panel about the business of professional speaking, where I shared some of the strategies I outlined in chapter 5, such as the importance of creating content in order to attract speaking inquiries.

At the in-person gathering, Port showcases his approach and best material, creates a feeling of group camaraderie and community, and is able to directly pitch his best customers—that is, existing ones—on future offerings that might interest them. That includes the "graduate program," which is an intensive $20,000 package in which students travel to Philadelphia and spend sixteen days in residence over a four-month period. Port rents out a theater with multiple performance spaces, and the students literally spend days at a time rehearsing. "We've modeled that on a conservatory," he says. In its first iteration, the program drew twenty participants. When you've built a dedicated fan base and bring them together, it can create powerful returns. Says Port, "When we announced it at the [Heroic Public Speaking] event, it sold out immediately."

He also believes it's important to keep your community interested by continually rolling out new opportunities. (And discontinuing some when they become stale, such as eliminating the in-person component of his mastermind program, as discussed previously, in chapter 4 on coaching and consulting.) "When people see the same offerings, they start to get bored," he says. "But if you throw in something they've never seen before, they go, 'Oh, what's that one?'"

One new initiative he decided to launch in the summer of 2016 was a five-day retreat for aspiring authors, along with his friend Mike Michalowicz (who founded the speakers' referral group that Port and I both participated in). They rented three estates on the Chesapeake Bay, and twenty participants gathered each day to roll up their sleeves and work on their book or book proposals. The price was steep—$10,000 a head—but so was the value proposition: at the end of the week, participants would have finally completed their proposals.

Creating a new offering, says Port, "will keep people paying attention. Every year, we'll have one or two different things in there that don't require an enormous amount of content development," because Port is focusing on subjects—like book writing—in which he's very experienced. "If it works really well, we'll do it again," he says. (Hosting live events isn't necessarily an easy way to make money, however. For some thoughts about the difficulties that might arise, see the sidebar "The Challenges of Live Events.")

Try This:

As you consider options for in-person events, ask yourself:

- What topics are people constantly asking you for help with? Are those topics amenable to being taught through a live event?

- What existing offerings do you have that you feel may have grown stale over the years? Is there something you should think about retiring?

- What new one or two offerings or events could you launch this year? How will you determine if your audience is interested (email survey, focus group discussion, offer a pilot, etc.)?

The Challenges of Live Events

Today, Jordan Harbinger is a well-known podcaster, thanks to his show the *Art of Charm*, which focuses on how to effectively use body language, persuasion, and charisma. (Initially, the show centered on dating and relationships, but has evolved into emphasizing how those skills can be deployed in a professional context.)

In the late 2000s, however, before podcasting became popular, Harbinger was just a young Wall Street lawyer with a side hobby. To his surprise, he recalls, "I started getting emails like, 'Hey, can you guys teach me in person the stuff you're talking about on the show?'" Harbinger recounts, "I was like, 'No, I work on Wall Street. I don't have time for this.'" But after enough entreaties, he relented.

Harbinger and his partner initially charged $100 for an afternoon session. But after a rebuke from a friend in business school who urged them to charge more, they began raising their prices. Today, the program has evolved into a weeklong, residential program in Los Angeles that costs between $6,000 and $8,000 to attend.

The margins on in-person events can be enticingly large. But, Harbinger cautions, it's not an easy way to make money. "I love live training; my coaches love live training," he says. "But there's tons more overhead than people think. You have to hire people that aren't going to quit, flake, steal from you, or drop the ball and give your customers a bad experience because they're not owners. You have to be around to do it at specific times. If you get sick, you need to replace yourself or that person, same as with any type of performance. People are really counting on you to overdeliver. It's great, but the problem is that scalability is low and very difficult."

Harbinger has built an enormously successful seven-figure business. But even so, "If I had to do it all over again, I would figure out any way possible to not do live training," he says. "I think probably every boot camp that we run, every single week, somebody's flight gets delayed, so we've got to control for that. One of our instructors is sick. Something broke that needs replacing, whether it's a bed in the place where people are sleeping, or the grill, so they can't cook. You've got to deal with that."

Occasional live events can be a gratifying way to augment your business. John Corcoran, the attorney who has been so successful with affiliate marketing, has organized a couple of high-end retreats with a price point of $4,000 per person. "I just really enjoy doing it and I think it complements some of the other work that I do," he says. "I enjoy traveling and don't get to travel as much as I did before I had kids, so I dream of these amazing locations," like Austin and Napa, where he's held events. He intends to plan future gatherings in his own bucket-list spots, including Cuba and Necker Island, Richard Branson's private getaway.

But Harbinger's model, with regular batches of new attendees arriving onsite every week, can be draining over time. "I don't necessarily recommend people start live training businesses," he advises. "There's just too much going on. It's tough to make it . . . Look, there are a lot of other ways to earn a living. Don't try to do this. It's too hard." Even Corcoran has decided to stop offering his retreats as one-offs, and now includes them as part of a broader mastermind group he's organizing, which makes planning and filling the slots less onerous.

Live events can be fun—and lucrative. But before you start to plan one, be realistic about the logistics involved and make sure you're fully prepared.

In this chapter, we've explored the power of bringing together your followers for various types of live events. In-person experiences are an incomparable form of community building, but the logistical challenges can prompt talented professionals to wonder: Isn't there an easier way to create a meaningful learning experience? That's where online courses come in—the subject of the next chapter.

How to Start Your Own Paid Mastermind Group

Liz Scully is an Irishwoman raised in Pakistan who is now location-independent, splitting her time between New York, London, and Colorado. She makes a full-time living by running mastermind groups that help business owners tackle their biggest challenges, both on her own and working for high-end authors and entrepreneurs who want to outsource the day-to-day facilitation of the masterminds they sponsor. Over the past five years that she's been organizing them, she's developed numerous strategies and best practices for how to launch an effective group. According to Scully, you have to make sure you get the following things right.

The right size. Masterminds don't have to be—and often shouldn't be—very large. "My preferred size for a mastermind is about four people," says Scully, "but I run between three and six [people]." For her clients, she's willing to run groups as large as eight, but "that's pushing it a bit" because she wants to be sure everyone has time to speak and be heard during the meetings.

The right frequency. There's no perfect frequency for mastermind groups to meet; it depends on the needs of the group. Scully prefers having group meetings (two-hour webinar chats, which people can access from anywhere in the world) every two weeks. "That's because that gives you enough time to set goals and then actually do them," she says. Some types of groups benefit from very regular check-ins—for instance, if you're all trying to write books or lose weight, weekly meetings can hold you accountable for your progress. But for very senior professionals, the focus of the group is likely to be on strategy, and that can't be turned around in a week or two; monthly meetings might be more appropriate.

The right price point. "Most masterminds that are professionally run [charge] between $500 and $2,000 a month," says Scully—thus, between $6,000 and $24,000 per year. Depending on the price point, this typically includes between one and three in-person meetings per year, as well as regular calls or webinars. If you're interested in starting one, it's not a bad idea to run a heavily discounted "beta version" in exchange for feedback, testimonials, and referrals. But once you get going, having a low price point can actually harm your business. If you work with corporate clients, says Scully, "then having a mastermind that's $1,000 for three months is not going to impress anyone. It's going to devalue your whole brand." Levesque took this approach to heart with his $35,000 mastermind group, which is steadily working up to a $50,000-per-year price point. Indeed, Scully has seen some elite mastermind groups cost up to $100,000 per year, though at higher price points, "you tend to get more than just a mastermind . . . You get training, you get one-to-one coaching, you get a retreat. It's a whole package."

The right people. Most important of all is having the right mix of people in your group, because if you've assembled people with wildly disparate goals or incompatible personalities, the group may fracture or fall apart. First, says Scully, focus on their goals. Having similar goals is important for focus and camaraderie; if one person wants to bring his business to $1 million a year and the other wants to lose fifty pounds, there may not be a lot that they can learn from one another in this context. Just a bit of difference is essential, however; your members are unlikely to want to share private financial information or trade secrets with direct competitors in their space.

Timing is also critical. Even if both parties want to earn $1 million a year, they have to be on relatively similar trajectories; someone who is making $800,000 now is likely to have very different needs and experiences than someone who is just launching his business and has barely brought in his first dollar. Personalities also matter. "If you had eight introverts in a mastermind, no one would speak," says Scully. "Likewise, with eight extroverts, no one would stop speaking." Don't simply accept everyone who is interested. "I typically turn away between 30 percent and 40 percent," she says. That doesn't mean she won't work with them ever, but that they're simply not a good fit for the current group.

Fixing a bad dynamic. You've worked hard to assemble a great group, but inevitably, mistakes sometimes happen, or people's life circumstances change. "Quick action is important," says Scully. "If it's beginning to go south, it's not going to get any better without jumping in." If it's apparent right away that someone isn't a fit, you as the leader need to speak with them to see how they're feeling and determine if they want to, or can, change their behavior or if it's simply better to let them go. "It's brave to do that because you obviously have to refund the money," she says. "Particularly if the money's $25,000, it's hard to say, 'You're not a good fit—sorry.' But it's going to be much better for you [and the group] long term."

New members aren't the only ones who can go astray. Sometimes a heretofore reliable group member might stop attending meetings, or consistently be late, or somehow disrupt the proceedings. "I would take that person aside and find out what's going on," says Scully. "It's normally about one of three things. It's a divorce, it's sickness, or it's financial problems. Almost always." Similarly, you'll need to determine whether the person can remedy the situation or if they need to leave.

Experience a mastermind group yourself. One rookie mistake Scully sees surprisingly often is professionals who want to launch a mastermind group of their own, yet have never even participated in one. "It's a bit like deciding to run a marathon when you've never run for a bus," she says. By experiencing a mastermind as a group member, you can develop your own sensibility and decide which practices you enjoy or want to avoid replicating. You can also get firsthand experience with group dynamics and how to spot impending problems. The experience enables you to make informed decisions about the community you'd like to create.

Launching without a list. It's a lot easier to fill a mastermind with qualified participants when you have a robust list of followers to choose from. But even if you don't, Scully says that shouldn't deter you. Start by mapping out a precise vision of what you want the mastermind group to look like, and who you want to serve. Scully says, "The best way to fill a mastermind is to get clear on who it's for. Write a list of your ideal person or people . . . that are a really good fit. Then call them up and offer it to them. It's as simple as that." That actually might not sound simple at all—do you really know half a dozen people who would pay you thousands of dollars to join a mastermind group? But it's worked for Scully herself, who launched a $5,000 program to a list of forty-two people, and got five yeses. She also has a client who earns more than $500,000 per year from her mastermind groups alone, and her email list is fewer than 250 people.

Remember also that other people can help you build your email list through referrals. The clearer you are on your ideal customer, the more likely others can help you find them. That was certainly the case for Selena Soo, whose more than $20,000 annual publicity-focused mastermind group was mentioned in chapter 4. As she explains, "I made a list of all the people that I knew who I felt like were connected to my ideal client"—meaning good referral sources. She explained that she was looking for already successful professionals who wanted to learn how to increase their media exposure and public profile.

For instance, she called up a contact who ran a website focused on personal development, self-help, and health and, as a consequence, knew many successful professionals who contributed to the site. Soo said, "I got on the phone with him and people like him, and said, 'I'm opening up this mastermind and I'm really excited about it. This is what we're doing and I'm curious if you know anyone.'" She found her mastermind participants almost exclusively through referrals, including one from me, because she had so clearly articulated to me the kind of client she was looking for. Referrals are a powerful strategy because unless you have a very large or very targeted list, you likely won't have enough people in your immediate orbit who can afford the high-end price point.

Try This:

If you're thinking seriously about launching a mastermind group, ask yourself:

- What does the ideal mastermind group that you'd like to create look like? How many (and what kind of) people, meeting with what frequency, at what price point? Would it be entirely virtual or would you also include an in-person component?

- Think about where you can find your initial members. (If you've already hosted a Mastermind Day, that will be a good trial balloon; you know those people are interested in connecting with like-minded professionals.) Who else do you know with connections in the community you want to serve? Can they send you referrals?

PART THREE

Extend Your Reach and Impact Online

CHAPTER 9

Leverage Your Platform by Creating an Online Course

For many entrepreneurs, creating an online course is a natural step toward extending your reach and impact. But as some have learned the hard way (myself included), creating and launching a course can be a *real* learning process.

In this chapter, I'll share stories of successes—and failures—from which you can derive a number of key lessons, including the importance of understanding what your customers want; testing your assumptions; listening to your audience; crafting a compelling narrative; surveying your audience; launching a pilot; pricing your course (including at premium levels); and finally, mastering your first launch.

Understand What Your Customers Want

The subject line was hard to ignore: "Paying you $1K–$25K+ for a few hrs of your time." I might have deleted it as spam, but I knew the sender: Jared Kleinert, an ambitious fellow author who—at nineteen years old—had published a book about rising young entrepreneurs and future leaders.

"I'm looking at potentially creating my first information product centered around helping people find financial freedom," he wrote me. "I'd like you to be 1 of 10 chosen thought leaders to interview in a possible information product, and I'd pay you at minimum $1K for your time, as well as split commissions 50–50 with you as a joint venture partner if you'd like to help promote the course." How can any rational person turn that down?

So I said yes, along with podcaster John Lee Dumas and others. Course participants, the idea went, would get a dozen in-depth lessons about various ways they could monetize, from podcasting to video blogging on YouTube to (in my case) networking.

But a few months later, things hadn't quite worked out as planned. As Kleinert later wrote in an unusually transparent *Forbes* blog post:

> $997. $11,000. $0.
>
> The first number represents the retail cost to sign up for a course called Yourself with Wealth that I opened registration for two weeks ago. The second number is the amount I agreed to pay (in total) to my various partners and course instructors for 10 separate hour-long interviews as well as editing for four different videos used to help sell the course.

The final number is the amount of total sales I had after the 4 day launch period. Talk about a massive failure.[1]

What went so wrong? Online courses can be a fantastic way to monetize your expertise. But as Kleinert's experience shows, there's also a danger—the lure of the quick hit. "I think, as entrepreneurs, we like to chase the shiny object a lot," he says, "like a cool internet marketing course where you kind of throw some numbers in your head and think you can make six figures in two months."

Kleinert thought his idea had promise. People were clearly interested in how to make money online; it was a booming industry. Thanks to his strong network, he could tap an impressive lineup of expert instructors, and with their followings, he could potentially reach a large audience.

But, he realized later, he had missed a vital step. "I never interviewed any potential customers," he says. "All that I totally skipped, because I was in such a rush to make a quick buck." It didn't help that he launched just before Thanksgiving in the United States, when many potential customers would have been distracted by travel or family obligations, or saving up for holiday presents. And, he realized, his offer to pay participants ending up being counterproductive. They said yes quickly—who doesn't want $1,000 for an hour of their time?—but weren't particularly invested in promoting it to their audience, as they would have been if that were their only source of revenue.

In some regards—like overall sales—Kleinert's venture was indeed a failure. But he also did some things right. For one, he kept costs down. His launch budget was minimal, only a few hundred dollars in software and video editing costs. He only promised the $1,000 interview fee upon completion of each interview, so when sales didn't come through, he wasn't on the hook for those costs.

Even more critically, to use the Silicon Valley parlance, he "failed fast." He says, "I found a way to test an internet marketing idea, an online course, in probably six weeks, whereas most people would spend six months or a year getting this project together and trying to sell it." Instead of meticulously building out the product and then launching it, he attempted to sell it before it was built, and when it didn't attract any takers, he was able to shut it down quickly.

Instead of burying his defeat and silently slinking away, he went public, sharing what he learned in his *Forbes* piece. "The second I published it, everyone was saying how vulnerable it was, and how transparent it was," he says. "There's no reason not to be vulnerable . . . I think it's a strength. I think it attracts respect from people."

Kleinert has moved on to other business ventures, including a new book. But he's taken the lessons with him. "You have to build up over time," he says. "You have to ask your customers what they want. You need to build something that's of value to them, and scale that over time."

Test Your Assumptions

If your goal is to launch a course, not selling any is depressing. But there's actually something far worse, and that's selling only *one*. In 2010, Montreal-based entrepreneur Danny Iny decided to launch his own online course, a magnum opus called "Marketing That Works." But the title quickly proved ironic, because sales were abysmal. Iny says, "We launched this thing . . . and one person bought it. For the next six months, every freaking week, it was like, I'm on the clock to finish creating another lesson for this one guy."

Looking back, he says, "I worked six months of my life for $1,000. I didn't want to do that again." He began searching for opportunities to promote the course. Maybe, he thought, guest posting on other people's blogs could work. He pitched an article to the prominent website *Copyblogger*, and it was a hit: more than two hundred comments and nine hundred tweets. Most importantly, it drove traffic back to his own website, so Iny began to believe that perhaps it really could drive course sales. He decided to double down.

He began pitching dozens of other prominent blogs, and almost all said yes. Within a year, he had written guest posts for more than eighty sites. "People started asking, 'How are you doing this? Can you teach me?'" he recalls. "When enough of these responses had come in unsolicited, I was like, 'OK, there's demand. Even though I feel like I've been burned before, I think I have to try doing this again.'" So Iny launched another online course about how to successfully guest blog. He called it "Write Like Freddy," a joking reference to a fan's comment about his ubiquity—that through his blogging, he seemed to be everywhere, just like the 1980s horror movie villain, Freddy Krueger.

But this time, he was going to make sure he wasn't running the course for an audience of one. Iny sent an email out to his list of a few thousand people, offering fifty slots in a pilot program. They could enter the course at a reduced price and receive more personal access to him, in exchange for providing detailed feedback as he developed the material in real time. "In hindsight, this actually is really brilliant marketing, but it's not because I was cooking up a brilliant idea," Iny says. "It was just trying to hedge my bets, so if nobody bought, I could walk away from it."

But this time—because the idea for the course had arisen organically from customer requests—the demand was there. Unlike his behemoth first effort, which encapsulated Iny's view of "everything that I knew people needed" about marketing, "Write Like Freddy" emerged as a shorter, tightly focused course on a narrow subject. Pilot enrollees paid $77, and the eventual price was $137; the course became a hit.

Listen to Your Audience

When you're forcing an idea on the market, like Kleinert's mashup of different monetization strategies, it can be hard—if not impossible—to find your audience. But sometimes, if you listen carefully, your community will ask for exactly what it wants, and what is normally an arduous process becomes a whole lot easier.

Scott Oldford had built a successful digital marketing agency, Infinitus. But his clients were paying for real-world services like copywriting, and that required staff and overhead. "In 2014, we really weren't able to profit off of a million dollars in revenue," he says. "I was doing fourteen-hour days, and I was like, 'There's something wrong here.'" He knew he needed to change his business model, but wasn't sure how.

Then, one day, his client's son had a request: "Scott, can you teach me everything you know about online marketing?" Oldford, who never went to college, was skeptical about his ability to teach, and demurred. But the young man pressed him: couldn't he reach out to his email list? If enough people wanted it, maybe Oldford would reconsider. So Oldford sent out a brief message: if he offered a program, would they be interested? "Three hours later, I had twenty-four slots, sold at $1,200 USD," he recalls.

Many online courses languish, the product of hopes and wishful thinking. But when you hit upon what your audience really wants, success can come fast.

Craft a Compelling Narrative

Once you have a good idea of what your audience wants, the next step is to market your product with a compelling narrative to draw in buyers. Legendary internet marketer Jeff Walker offers some good advice. (For more on Walker's story, see the sidebar "The Origins of the Online Launch.") At the heart of Walker's approach is what he dubs "The Sideways Sales Letter." For decades, direct-mail copywriters were renowned in the business world as being among the savviest and most effective marketers, crafting extremely long sales letters—sometimes dozens of pages—that drew in large numbers of buyers with their detailed, immersive storytelling. Walker's insight, fundamentally, was how to apply those strategies in the online era. At first, limited by the constraints of dial-up bandwidth, he simply created email versions of those in-depth sales letters. By 2000, he was able to incorporate audio messages, and a few years after that—as more and more people had access to broadband—he took to video.

He embraced the medium immediately. "If you had to make a sale, if your life depended on making that sale, then the best way to make that sale is to be sitting down with someone face-to-face and you could look into their eyes," he says. But one-to-one selling doesn't scale. Video, however, can at least come close.

He realized that what made direct marketing sales letters so compelling to consumers was their narrative. "It's about standing out from the market by delivering that value and doing it in a story-based way, because stories are how humans communicate,

The Origins of the Online Launch

For five years, Jeff Walker had been a stay-at-home dad caring for his two kids. But increasingly, his wife was feeling the strain of being the sole provider. "She was getting up in the dark and coming home in the dark, and working as hard as she could, and we were having a hard time making ends meet," he recalls. He knew he needed to find a way to help. His thoughts turned to the stock market, an obsession of his for years. It was 1996, and the internet was just starting to take off. "That was my dream, to become a trader and make all my money trading," he says. "My problem was, I didn't have any capital, any money. But I heard about this idea of publishing online."

Walker started a free email newsletter sharing his thoughts about the stock market, and he sent it to everyone he knew who had an email address—a whopping nineteen contacts. But it grew steadily through word of mouth, and within a few months, he'd managed to attract nearly fifteen hundred subscribers. "I had this thought that maybe I could sell them something," he says. "But I'd never sold anything in my life. I had no sales experience, no marketing experience. I was scared to ask for money."

But he needed to start earning to help with his family's finances, so on January 1, 1997, Walker launched a paid version of his newsletter—an early instance of the now-popular "freemium" model popular in Silicon Valley, in which all comers can access a basic model for free, but those who are particularly interested can upgrade to a paid version with more and better features.

"At first I couldn't take online payments," he recalls. "That was like rocket science back then. So I sent them a long email that said, 'If you want to get this paid thing, print this out and mail me a check,' and that's what they did." That first launch brought in $1,600—certainly not life-changing money, but an early indication that his concept could work.

About six months later, Walker launched the product again, publicizing the paid offer to his free subscribers and explaining the benefits. By that point, he'd improved his sales copy and had an actual product—the newsletter—to sell, rather than just the promise of creating one. This time, he took in $6,000. "That was a quantum leap," he says. Because he was selling an email newsletter, his fulfillment costs were zero, and his product was almost infinitely scalable: he'd discovered the path to pure profit.

For the next few years, Walker proceeded to grow his business, including a launch in early 2000 that brought in $106,000 in seven days. In 2003, he attended a marketing conference and was talking with his fellow attendees about his experiences. "I sort of figured everyone was doing what I was doing," he says. He was wrong. They were flabbergasted by his success and wanted to understand his techniques. That's when he began to shift away from his writing about the stock market and entered a new market: teaching others how to run profitable online launches.

Today, Walker's methodology, which he's dubbed the Product Launch Formula (PLF), has become ubiquitous in the world of online marketing. "It takes your marketing and turns it into an event, almost like a ritual, that captures people's attention," he says.

and they're incredibly captivating," he says. "If you take your marketing and turn it into a story-based event, it pulls people in."

The letters told a story in a logical progression that sparked initial interest and then pulled customers steadily along toward the decision to buy. They started with attention-grabbing headlines, then moved into a fascinating story, bullet points touting the benefits of the purchase, an explanation of the offer, information about the price and additional bonuses and guarantees you'd receive, and finally a closing ask for the sale.

With video, Walker realized, he could accomplish the same thing. But instead of drawing people in with *length*—that is, a really long sales letter—he could cultivate that interest and connection over *time*, in the form of a series of videos. He thought of it almost mathematically: in his mind, he was shifting the vertical axis of length to the horizontal axis of time. Thus, he created "The Sideways Sales Letter."

The first video would, in effect, be the headline. "It's all about the journey or the opportunity," he says. He explains how customers have a unique opportunity to transform their lives. In his case, the videos tout entrepreneurial opportunity, but others who follow the formula would highlight the transformational possibilities their own products or courses offered, such as the ability to get healthy and lose weight, or to finally master your golf game. Of course, it's essential that even the first video, while framing the journey, is informative and useful to the viewer, rather than simply a parade of beach shots and Ferraris, dangling the infuriating possibility of untold secrets that will be revealed—eventually.

The second video, Walker says, lays out the equivalent of a sales letter's bullet points. "This is where you're taking that transformation and you're making it real for them," he says. He lays out case studies—in his case, tied to entrepreneurs who have successfully used his Product Launch Formula (PLF)—and contains a strong educational component, as viewers are getting an overview of how to think about the subject he's teaching. He's demonstrating his mastery of the subject and offering value to them upfront, in the form of interesting information with no strings attached.

The third video, according to Walker, "gives them what's in [the program] and what's in it for them." This video is still educational and provides useful strategies, but begins to pivot subtly toward the sales offer, explaining "what we're actually selling them, what they'll actually get out of it, [and] what it will be like." At the end, there's a nod toward the fourth video—the sales video. They'd announce, "In your next video, we're going to tell you how to do this," explains Walker.

The first three videos have provided a healthy dose of inspiration, aspiration, and education. "The philosophy is that it's all about delivering big value before you ask for the sale," says Walker. You need to proceed gently over time, offering more information and knowledge, so that potential buyers' concerns are assuaged: they understand you're an expert, have already benefited from your teaching, and have gotten a taste of what it would be like to participate in your more in-depth program. The fourth video explains the offer in detail and makes the pitch explicitly.

This extended video sequence, says Walker, which is typically released over an approximately two-week period, is necessary to build trust when dealing with major purchases: "If you go buy a gallon of milk, there isn't a lengthy sales process." Not so if you're shopping for a Ferrari—and Walker's course, which sold for $2,000 in 2016, is the online equivalent. He also builds in an element of scarcity. Once the videos have been released, Walker lays out a short and clearly defined period of time, typically three to seven days, in which people are allowed to buy, which he dubs "cart open" and "cart close." That deadline, he says, gives people a compelling reason to purchase now, rather than deferring the decision indefinitely.

Walker's massive success—a recent launch of his PLF course brought in $5 million, and more than fifteen thousand people have been through the program—has enshrined his techniques as the default for many marketers, who fear that deviating from it will cost them sales. Indeed, Walker reports that his students have earned a collective $500 million in sales from their launches.

Of course, the standardization of his approach creates problems of its own. Though video is a personal medium that lets you speak directly to your audience, it can be hard to stand out when seemingly every other online marketer is using the same sequence and tactics.

Walker isn't concerned; if you harness storytelling properly, he feels, it taps into the fundamental nature of how humans relate and see the world. With more than two decades of experience in online marketing, he's honed his craft well; his recent launch videos can run as long as forty-five minutes, an eternity for a distractible, internet-era audience. But he's confident that going deep, rather than turning off viewers, will entice them further, and he has the experience to back it up. The question is how well others, using the same structure, can apply his principles. (For the story on my personal experience with launching products, see the sidebar "My Early Experiments.")

Survey Your Audience

Ryan Levesque, who runs high-level mastermind groups, came to prominence through developing his "Ask" methodology, which advocates surveying your customers before trying to sell them anything. So that's what I did.

In December 2015, I sent an email to my list, then numbering about 25,000 people. The headline was designed to get attention: "quick question," with no caps, so it looked as personal as possible. In email marketing, you can't overuse that trick—people will become upset and wary—but for the most important messages, it can be powerful. A full 10,700 people opened the email—an extraordinarily high open rate of 43 percent, compared to industry averages of 20 percent to 25 percent—and more than 1,200 took the time to fill out a detailed, ten-question survey.

The survey began with what Levesque says is the most critical question of all: "What's your single biggest professional challenge right now?" That allows respondents to answer in any way they'd like, unbiased by your subsequent line of questioning. You may have fixed ideas about their struggles, but this initial query allows you insight into what messaging and products will prove most salient for them. I then asked some basic demographic questions (age, gender, and whether they were entrepreneurs or worked inside a company) and asked them to rate which topics that I wrote about (such as personal branding, becoming a recognized expert, networking, etc.) were most appealing to them.

The results were fascinating. First, developing a reputation as a recognized expert was the most popular topic among my readers. A full 20 percent of respondents identified that as their number-one interest among a set of options listed, five percentage points higher than any other topic. That was interesting evidence, but, Levesque warns, not sufficient.

What you're looking for is not just overall sentiment; you're looking to identify the topics that *your most passionate fans* want. The way to identify that passion, he says, is to quantify the length of their responses; the longer their answers, the more invested they are in the topic. Indeed, if you're asking about their most pressing concern, it makes sense that the person

My Early Experiments

When I decided to launch my own online course, I tread carefully. By that time, I'd already had my share of costly failures when it came to launching products. For example, in the early days of my consulting business, I decided it would be smart to record some of my talks and have them printed as CDs and DVDs. The cost was close to $1,500. I could distribute some for free to heads of professional associations, who might book me to speak, and I could sell the rest at my events for $20 a pop. But before long, it became obsolete to send DVDs in the mail; anyone who was interested could view your videos online. And only three audience members ever ponied up to buy my CDs—four, if you count the man who asked for free copies in exchange for transcribing them and then never delivered. It was a lasting embarrassment, and I didn't want to repeat it.

So when I tried to launch my first online course in 2014, I signed on with a company that films and sells videos of you—at no charge to you—in exchange for an eighty-twenty split of sales proceeds (they take the lion's share). I didn't lose any money, but I barely made any. I earned a few thousand dollars in exchange for probably well over a hundred hours of planning, travel, and teaching time. But the experience became my laboratory, and I learned how the more well-established companies structured their online courses.

The following year, I tried another experiment, creating a much shorter course in partnership with a media company. This one only took me a day to create and film, compared to the massive time suck of the previous year. The returns were also quite modest—$1,000 or so in the first year—but with a much better return on investment than the first effort.

Listening to colleagues, however, I realized that the real secret was creating your own courses and reaping the profits directly. That could mean the difference between my $1,000 effort and the $150,000 that entrepreneur Selena Soo took home from her first online course launch in 2014. But I had to find the right topic—and that involved surveying my audience and then offering a pilot.

who answers simply "hiring" or "burnout" is less invested than the person who takes the time to write a deep and thoughtful answer.

Levesque also suggests something counterintuitive in this digital age: asking respondents for their phone number, and whether it would be OK to call them to follow up. Sometimes, you'll actually want to do this; you may have questions about their answer or want to dive deeper into the psychographics of an audience segment. But more often, this is simply a proxy question: if they say yes, it's also a clue that they're more interested and invested in you and your work. They are the people more likely to become your actual buyers, so it pays to weigh their responses more heavily.

It took weeks to review and catalog the free-form answers, but the data was invaluable. "I deeply want to be a thought leader," one person wrote. "Any further insight into building the 'thought' product would be very useful. I have some ideas around building a framework and grand narrative, but they need to be further refined and market tested. My dream would be to run this as a business full-time and give up my day job. I really want my natural strengths to be of service to others." Another expressed a wish for help with "sifting through the layers of bureaucracy in my large company to be recognized for my expertise through leadership and financial recognition."

In other words, I discovered there might be enough interest for a course on becoming a recognized expert, but I wasn't ready to launch even a pilot just yet. Instead, I reached out to fifty people who had indicated, per Levesque's suggested question, that they'd be willing to speak with me further. I didn't call them, however; instead, I emailed a request: Would they be willing to look at a one-page description of a course I was thinking of offering and let me know what they thought of it? There was nothing overtly in it for them; it was a pure favor. (Though I did later circle back and offer them the first chance to enroll in the pilot, if they wished to.) But if you've developed a trusting relationship over time with your readers, they'll often want to be helpful to you, as a way of paying you back for the value that your content has provided them.

I asked them whether they'd be interested in a course on how to become a recognized expert, what information would be most important to include in a course like that, and what they liked most and least in the course description I'd shared. I also asked if they'd be interested in signing up for the course if it cost $500 and why or why not. Fifteen people responded, and five said yes. As entrepreneur Bryan Harris shared in a podcast interview with Pat Flynn, if you can get 10 percent of your respondents to agree to buy from you, that's a strong indicator there's sufficient demand for your product, so I finally felt confident enough to launch my pilot.[2]

Offer a Pilot

Nearly five months after surveying my audience, I sent out another email, this one titled, "A Chance to Work with Me—Special Pilot Offer." In the text, I explained the specifics: I was opening up forty spots in a special pilot course on becoming a recognized expert that would consist of six live webinars over a five-week period. We'd cover topics ranging from "Finding Your Breakthrough Idea" to "Building a Powerful Network." In exchange for sharing frequent feedback about the course (and perhaps providing a testimonial afterward if they enjoyed it), participants would get more personal access to me and a much lower price: $500, instead of the $2,000 that the course would cost when it officially launched.

I conducted my pilot via a series of live webinars. But there are also many other variations you can use; the goal is to obtain in-depth feedback from a smaller group of participants so you can iterate as needed. As Danny Iny notes, "A pilot can be anything" from a live event to a series of coaching calls to an email course. "The bias should always be towards what you can deploy as quickly and easy as possible so you can get feedback."

I felt ready to try the experiment, but when you're launching something new, you can never be sure how it will be received. I tried to keep Iny's mantra in mind: "Piloting is going to go in the market research bucket," he says. "When you launch a pilot and it doesn't go great, that's not a bad sign. That's just a data point."

I was in the middle of teaching an executive education class when I scheduled the email to be sent. Forty-five minutes later, it was time for our lunch break, so I logged on to check my email. It was overflowing with unread messages, all of them purchases. We'd already more than sold out, and I had to shut down the sales page immediately. After wasting thousands of dollars in the past with half-baked ideas I hadn't properly vetted, I had finally figured out how to identify what my audience truly wanted. In less than an hour, I earned $23,500.

Try This:

As you're thinking about what topic to offer as a pilot course, ask yourself:

- What do others consistently ask your advice about (how to guest blog for other people's websites, or how to dress more fashionably, or how to be a better parent)? Would it be possible to systematize that knowledge and teach it as an online course?

- Write up a short description (half a page to a page in length). Now make a list of fifty people you think might be interested. Send it to them and ask for their thoughts and feedback, and ask if they'd be willing to buy it at the price point you've set. If at least 10 percent say yes, strongly consider offering the course.

Pilot Email

To download a free copy of the email I used to market my online pilot course, go to dorieclark.com/PilotEmail.

Price Your Course Right

In the world of online courses, there's enormous pricing variation. For as little as $14, you can take classes on how to "Become a Hadoop Developer" or "Build a Bigger and Gladiator Looking Chest" on sites like Udemy, which specializes in low-priced offerings. There's also a myriad of free alternatives—including taped versions of classes from top universities—on sites like edX. At the other end of the spectrum, it's common for online marketers to charge $2,000 for a course (both Danny Iny and Jeff Walker have courses in this range), and at the high end, entrepreneur Ramit Sethi offers a $12,000 course called "Dream Job Elite," which promises to teach enrollees skills in networking, interviewing, and salary negotiation.

So how do you know what to charge? As Iny puts it, "All prices exist on a spectrum, where at the very top is the most the market will bear, and at the very bottom is the least you can afford to charge and still not lose money. Everything in between is positioning." In other words, you can differentiate your course based on what your competitors are offering, the level of depth or experience you bring to the material, the level of support you'll offer, the results your participants can expect to get, and so on. It's of course impossible to promise specific results, but a course like Sethi's that shows you how to land your dream job and negotiate a higher salary has a clearer ROI than one that teaches you how to knit wool hats.

When it comes to pricing a pilot course, Iny suggests keeping two metrics in mind. First, what percentage of the full course will you be offering? (This is inexact, so you can insert your best guesstimate.) For instance, your material might be quite undeveloped, and you're heavily relying on course participants to shape it. In that case, you might be presenting 20 percent of the material your class will ultimately cover. If you're ultimately planning to charge $1,000, that implies a $200 price tag for the pilot.

However, there's also a second metric, which tips the scale in the opposite direction: your time and personal attention. Your audience will likely value the individual contact and may be willing to pay extra for it. For instance, in running my pilot program, I taught each session as a live weekly webinar, taking questions directly from participants. I also responded personally to their emails and interacted with them extensively in our private Facebook group, so the participants who wanted to get to know me personally definitely had the chance to do so.

I knew their names, personal biographies, and business challenges, and often shared very personal, specific tips, such as listening to their elevator pitch and suggesting how to modify it. That level of interaction simply wouldn't be possible with a large-scale course. Thus, I felt comfortable charging $500 for the pilot program, as I planned to offer the full course for between $1,500 and $2,000.

My earlier courses, done in partnership with other organizations, retailed for $100 or less. But for my own first offering, I decided to set a higher price point. It's not an easy decision; most of your audience, even if they wanted to, probably couldn't afford a $2,000 purchase from you. It feels more democratic and egalitarian to price your offerings lower, and it may limit snarky comments and disapprobation from some readers, who resent your efforts to monetize.

But the truth is, the moment you charge *anything*, some people will be displeased. As I recounted in my previous book, *Stand Out*, Sethi told me that, to this day, he's never been more nervous about a decision than when he launched his first paid product, a $4.95 ebook. Sure enough, even at that modest price point, he received hate mail calling him a sellout. So he's learned not to worry about it.

"Do you need to build your business with a $7 thing first, and a $77 thing second, and a $777 thing third? No, you don't," says Iny. "In fact, there's a really strong business logic argument to start with higher-priced stuff when you're small, because the economics work out better." As he points out, if you have a fifty-thousand-person email list, you can make great money by selling a $200 product. But if you only have five hundred subscribers, even if you sold to an eye-popping 10 percent of your audience, you'd only make $10,000—nice, but certainly not enough to live on. (In actuality, sales conversion rates ranging from 0.5 percent to 2 percent of your list are far more common.)

Explore Premium Pricing

Selena Soo, the business and publicity strategist, took the same approach with her online efforts (see chapter 4). In May 2014, she launched a premium-priced online course called "Get Known, Get Clients," which cost $3,000 if you paid in full, or $3,500 broken into monthly increments. For a first-time course creator with a relatively modest following—only thirty-eight hundred on her email list at the time—it was a bold move. "People told me you shouldn't launch something at that price point," she recalls. "No one's going to buy it."

Cost wasn't the only obstacle. Instead of following the traditional pattern of developing a two-month-long course, Soo's lasted a full half-year. "I knew I was taking a risk," she says, "but at the same time, I just knew that to fulfill that promise to really help people build a foundation for their own six-figure business,

I couldn't just give them a four-week or an eight-week course and call it a day."

Soo didn't just set an arbitrary price point and cross her fingers, however. Despite its high price tag, she had every reason to believe the course would succeed because of the meticulous plan she'd laid out. She wasn't trying to launch her business with the online course. She had already created a six-figure business and steady cash flow—and had validated the concepts she taught—through developing a one-on-one coaching practice and her elite mastermind group.

Planning a Premium Course

No matter how compelling your audience finds your work, of course, there are only so many people who can afford a $20,000-plus program. Soo knew there was pent-up demand: "People would say, 'I'm saving up to work with you one day,' or ask, 'Do you have other kinds of offerings?'" So when she decided to launch an online course, she had the advantage of already having a high price anchor in people's minds. "When I launched the $3,000 offering, it seemed very cheap to certain people," she says.

Now she needed to choose the right topic. Again, instead of simply launching blindly, she followed a series of logical steps. "I actually wanted to create a networking product at first," she recalls. She sent out a survey to understand her audience's aspirations and challenges around networking, and then, as Levesque recommends, followed up with those who indicated they'd be willing to talk further. "I said, 'I'm thinking of doing this course and would probably price it at $297. You'd get A, B, and C. What do you think?' The response was lukewarm. I was like, *what's the point of me creating this if people aren't excited about it?*" she says.

So she started to consider other options. Networking had been a topic she was interested in teaching. But what were her students proactively requesting? "I knew that everybody was looking to get known and to get clients to build their business, because they needed revenue," she says. "That was the number-one thing for people. Just by listening to the market and testing different things, I realized, *this is what I'm going to do*."

But before she went deeper, she needed to test the premise yet again. People would regularly email her to ask if there was a way, besides her top-tier mastermind group, that they could work together. She started to call them up and float the idea of her new course. She tested the price point, saying that she'd likely offer it at between $3,000 and $4,000. Would they be interested? The response, she recalls, was overwhelmingly positive: "People were like, "Yeah, I'm very interested. That's exactly what I need.""

Soo was very familiar with Jeff Walker's launch techniques, which she describes as "amazing." But she felt she didn't have time to make an elaborate series of hyper-polished videos. "I just chose to throw myself into it, versus waiting until everything was perfect and I had everything outlined, and every script written out," she says. "I think that in business, if you're going to reach your full potential, you can't wait. You just have to take action." Where you need to invest time is in getting the fundamental concept right. In her case, she was confident that "Get Known, Get Clients" would sell, so now she needed to get it on the market.

Master Your First Launch

After deciding not to do videos, Soo's path was clear. She'd launch to her thirty-eight hundred email subscribers through a combination of emails and a live webinar presenting the concepts in the course. She leveraged the power of scarcity to drive sign-ups: "I told people this is the only webinar I'm doing this year," she says, and she wasn't going to circulate a replay. Nearly a thousand signed up for her webinar, and half attended live.

For those who didn't attend, however, she had created a series of emails that reiterated key principles—her three big ideas—about the topics she had discussed live. All drove home the central message about the importance of raising your profile in order to get clients, and how to do it. "I made sure that the quality of the webinar and the emails were really epic," she says. "Then afterwards, I would share social proof like, 'These people signed up for the program . . .' There were a whole series of emails, but it didn't really take that long to do compared to what could have been four times the amount of work [with videos]."

More people can afford a $3,000 course than a $20,000-plus program, to be sure. But it's still not accessible to most. When it comes to premium online courses, this is never going to be a volume business, and you have to get comfortable with low conversion rates. However, even a few sales can add up quickly. Targeting just a few of the right customers can create robust profits. With her first launch—a webinar and a few emails—Soo sold fifty enrollments in "Get Known, Get Clients." "That was over 1 percent, which is considered high, so I made $150,000 in that first launch," she says. On its own, that's a handsome salary for most professionals, and it's even more impressive when you keep in mind that was only a portion of her overall income.

She upgraded her business model first from one-on-one coaching to group coaching. But after several launches of "Get Known, Get Clients," she realized that was the path forward.

She stopped offering her mastermind group in 2016, and moving forward, she plans to focus on online courses.

Try This:

As you consider how to structure your course, think about the results that your clients need and ask yourself:

- How long, realistically, will it take for them to see results? Can they learn the material by themselves, such as through video modules? Or do they need more intensive involvement from you, or from a peer group?

- Write down in detail what the most effective course you could offer would look like. What will you teach them, when, and how?

- What price point would make this a win from your perspective? Do you know people, or could you activate a referral stream of people who could afford to pay? Even if the numbers are high, like Soo's course, some will opt in if they trust you and perceive sufficient value.

CHAPTER 10

Create Digital Products and Online Communities

Once you've built an economic base for yourself with high-level offerings such as coaching and online courses, you might find it worthwhile to create lower-priced alternatives such as ebooks and virtual summits. Ideally you're expanding your following over time, so as your audience grows, it becomes increasingly possible to make a decent profit from $100 or even $10 products. Even with a small audience, some die-hard fans desperately want to buy something from you, but just can't afford a $2,000–3,000 course. Why not give them another option?

Jason Van Orden of *Internet Business Mastery* thinks of these varied product offerings as an "ascension ladder." It's foolish to only think about selling big-ticket courses and then moving on, he says. Instead, you have to focus on your *customer lifetime value.*

Think about it: Once someone has purchased from you, what else might they be interested in buying? What other products or services do they need? If someone can afford an expensive course, they can certainly afford a cheaper product, and they've already demonstrated that they're interested in your approach. Why not find ways you can continue to help them? A marquee course, he says, "is just the first thing, the baseline thing they sign up for. There's always going to be additional needs that we can fulfill by selling them."

In this chapter, we'll explore how to create lower-cost offerings including ebooks, virtual summits, subscription services, and online communities.

Create an Ebook

One popular low-dollar product, which is easy to create and sell, is an ebook. That's the approach Steve "SJ" Scott took. In September 2012, Scott—who had previously focused on online and affiliate marketing—decided to double-down on self-publishing books via Amazon.com. He has now written more than forty, pumping out a short book of 15,000–25,000 words about every three weeks.[1]

They were earning him a solid income, but his fortieth book—*Habit Stacking: 97 Small Life Changes That Take Five Minutes or Less*—became a best-seller. Fueled by its success, and the fact that eager readers had a huge backlist of his books they could purchase, his income skyrocketed and he's earned as much as $40,000 per month through his self-publishing.[2]

But there are also disadvantages to self-publishing. Amazon doesn't release the names or contact information of your buyers to you, for instance. That means, if you want to connect with your readers, you'll need to be strategic. Scott, for instance, includes links in his ebooks to additional information that readers might want. The additional resources are located on his website, where he encourages readers to opt in to his email list.[3]

Another disadvantage to self-publishing is that Amazon has set typical pricing standards for ebooks; no one really expects to pay more than $10 or $15, at most. If you want to create valuable content with premium pricing, you'll need to self-publish (even a simple PDF will sometimes do) and sell through your own website, using a service like E-Junkie or Gumroad to process sales. You'll need to drive traffic on your own, unlike Amazon, where existing customers may stumble upon your work through a keyword search. But you'll be able to charge higher prices, creating the possibility of substantial profit.

That's what Pat Flynn discovered with the initial ebook on green building certification he posted for sale online in 2008. He offered it through his own website for $19.99 a copy, and in his first month, he earned $7,908.55. "This was [what I earned doing] two-and-a-half months of architecture work, in one month of doing online business," he says. "And not only that. It was semi-automated, so people could go to the site, download and purchase the book, and it would automatically get delivered to them. I was just at home and I would literally wake up with more money in my PayPal account, which was just insane to me."

Hearing those numbers might inspire you to write your own ebook ASAP, and you may well get some buyers. But it's unlikely you can replicate Flynn's eye-popping sales numbers out of the gate. He had built trust with his audience over time by blogging for free, so they already knew his information was solid, making them far more likely to order a copy. And his regular blog posts had contributed to a robust Google ranking, driving new people to discover his work. If you're starting from scratch, building your readership will take time.

Once you do, however, ebooks can drive significant revenue. That's what Bjork and Lindsay Ostrom also discovered. Lindsay's ebook on food photography, priced at $29, has sold more than 7,600 copies, creating a revenue stream of more than $220,000—a *lot* bigger than most book advances from traditional publishers these days. (Exact numbers are hard to come by, but in 2011, only 6 percent of books were reported to have gotten six-figure advances, and it's almost certain that the numbers have decreased since then.[4])

Flynn and the Ostroms priced their ebooks at the lower end of the spectrum, analogous to many hardcover books. That's a viable choice, and customers generally won't complain. But if you offer specialized or highly coveted information (especially with a clear ROI, such as how to increase your income), you can also price your ebook more aggressively.

For instance, freelance writer Alexis Grant offers a $47 ebook on how to *Turn Your Side Hustle into a Full-Time Business and Surpass Your Day Job Income in Just Six Months*.[5] Depending on your niche and your positioning, some entrepreneurs have charged closer to $100 or $150 for their ebooks, though as you ascend to higher levels of pricing, it becomes harder to justify the value of "just" a book, since the $10–$30 price point is so firmly established in people's heads. If you want to increase the perceived value of your product, add in other modalities, such as checklists, case studies, or videos.

That's what Navid Moazzez learned when he launched *The Branding Summit* in 2014.

Organize Virtual Summits

Moazzez, an aspiring online entrepreneur from Sweden, had only a thousand email subscribers, and he wanted to increase both his public profile and his network. He realized that hosting a virtual summit—what he calls a "podcast on steroids"—could help him accomplish both. While a podcast is ongoing, a summit is a onetime event typically featuring video interviews with twenty to thirty leading thinkers.

Attracted by a time-limited opportunity to watch the interviews for free, interested fans opt in with their email address and, in return, gain access to those videos for a certain period of time, usually twenty-four to seventy-two hours. If they want to watch the videos after that, they can pay a modest fee—typically somewhere between $100 and $300—for lifetime access.

If he did it right, Moazzez knew, he could use the summit as a way to make connections and build relationships, and also to grow his email list dramatically because many of the participants might promote it to their own audiences. So in 2014, he began conducting interviews for *The Branding Summit*, a series of online video interviews about marketing and branding with well-known authors and experts (I was one of the interviewees).

Here's how Moazzez did it. First, he took a strategic approach, identifying the people he wanted to interview and building relationships with them well in advance of his ask. "Think about what you can do to add value to them before you even reach out," he says. "There are so many ways. You can leave thoughtful comments on their blogs, share their content. If they're an author, leave an Amazon review. Or even better, a video review, because authors never get video reviews." (He's right.)

Next, when he felt comfortable that he'd established a solid connection with a potential interviewee, he made the ask. Once they did the interview, he asked them to suggest high-level friends who might be a fit for the summit; this allowed him to approach people he didn't know with a warm introduction. Indeed, my friend Susan RoAne, author of *How to Work a Room*, initially connected me to Moazzez.

Contrary to what some might expect with his interview requests, Moazzez started at the top. "I decided to focus on getting some A-listers, a few really on the top, so that I could leverage off their credibility," he says. "Then I got B- and C-listers, as I like to call them. What I mean by that is that they have a good-sized audience and some are up-and-comers, but they still have a passionate audience of a few thousand people on their email list."

His plan was savvy: extremely famous experts might not be willing to email their list about the summit, regarding it as too small to bother. But they served an even more valuable purpose: their presence in the summit gave it legitimacy, and rising stars were eager to be associated with their more well-known colleagues. (*I'm going to be featured in an online summit alongside John Lee Dumas and Danny Iny!*")

As Moazzez surmised, those were the people motivated to promote the summit on his behalf; even if they only reached a few thousand people, those numbers added up. Moazzez worked to *ensure* they added up; he interviewed an astonishing eighty-eight people for the summit, more than double the typical size of a virtual summit. He ultimately gained three thousand new email subscribers and made $20,000 in profit from sales of all-access passes to the summit. "This enabled me to quit my job and move abroad"—as he told me during a Skype call from Cancún, where he was residing at the time.

Some imitators try so hard to leverage the value of summits that they actually require participants to sign agreements pledging to promote it to their email lists. Moazzez finds the approach heavy-handed, and I agree. If the content of the summit is interesting enough, and the speakers compelling enough, then participants will *want* to promote it, and that's far better than forcibly compelling them to do so. I turn down all requests to participate in summits that have strings attached.

Moazzez's success with his summit led to media coverage and a flurry of inquiries from aspiring entrepreneurs. *How, exactly, had he done it?* Vowing to teach others the right way to approach the process, he began to take on coaching clients and created a course, the Virtual Summit Mastery Program. In spring 2016, he had his first six-figure launch, bringing in more than $180,000.

Moazzez isn't the only one who's had tremendous success monetizing virtual summits. Michael Stelzner, of *Social Media Examiner* blog and podcast fame, grew his email list and his business by creating a steady stream of great content about the emerging world of social media. "I knew if I could build a list of ten thousand email subscribers, then I could begin monetizing," he says. "And the way that I was going to monetize was to create the 2010 Social Media Success Summit." Summits were a relatively new concept at the time, and Stelzner assembled an array of bold-faced names. They drew twelve hundred paid attendees and "it generated hundreds and hundreds of thousands of dollars," he says. The concept worked so well, he expanded it. "We got to the point where we were doing three a year, one in February, one in May, and one in October," he recalls. "We did $1.7 million in the first calendar year with that strategy."

But as with all good things, there are limits. "We found you can only promote so many things before your audience becomes fatigued," he says. He eventually cut back to one summit per year. That's why, when it comes to digital products, it pays to consider multiple revenue streams and different business models you can deploy as needed. One of the best models, online entrepreneurs have discovered, involves developing a recurring revenue stream, such as an online subscription service.

Try This:

As you start to investigate virtual summits, consider the following:

- Register for at least two to three virtual summits to see what they're like, how they're promoted, how the interviews are conducted, and how sales on the back end are run. (If you subscribe to the email lists of influencers in your field, you'll likely find out about various virtual summits they're involved in organically, but if not, simply Google the term and you'll find a variety for which you can sign up.)

- If you'd like to create a virtual summit, identify your topic of choice. I've participated in virtual summits focused on everything from peak personal performance to self-publishing to how to become an authority in your field.

- Create a list of the forty to fifty people you'd most like to land as interviews. Sort them into "A" and "B" lists—household names versus those who are well regarded but lesser known. Which A-listers do you have a connection to? Are there people you already know, or could get a warm introduction to? If not, start now and work on building a relationship with them through things like writing an online review of their book or starting to share their posts on social media.

- When the moment feels right (i.e., you have a warm introduction, the influencers have taken note of you, and/or you've been doing online relationship-building activities for a while), approach them with your ask and see if you can land at least three A-list interviews, which can serve as an anchor for your summit.

- Now go down your ideal interviewee list and, mentioning the A-listers' involvement, issue your interview requests. You'll ideally land between twenty and thirty overall. Schedule them and start creating your marketing materials (for your own audience, and for your participants to share with theirs). Ideally, your launch will dramatically grow your email list and perhaps provide some revenue, as well.

Build a Subscription Service

Andrew Warner, the online entrepreneur who succeeded wildly with online greeting cards and failed miserably with online invitations, founded his video-interview website *Mixergy* to answer his own questions about entrepreneurship. But, eventually, he says, "I wanted the business to support itself so I wasn't making the same mistake again by just throwing money at another idea." He toyed with the idea of accepting ads, but ultimately concluded that "I'd like people to actually like this so much that they'd be willing to pay for it." There was only one way to find out.

Today, *Mixergy* operates on a freemium model. All new interviews are free for anyone to watch for a week, but after that, they're only available to paid *Mixergy* members, with fees of $25 per month or $199 per year.

That broad, free initial exposure—Warner has an email list of seventy thousand subscribers—is inducement for prominent figures to agree to an interview. And the deadline, he realized, provided a powerful reason for free listeners to actually download his material, bolstering his iTunes ranking. He says, "There's so much coming at us online, why bother reading a blog post? Why bother downloading another podcast? . . . There's no incentive . . . unless you know that if you don't do it, then it's going to go to premium members only. In which case, you'll go in and grab it as fast as possible."

When it comes to monetizing, people who are very interested in hearing a certain interviewee and who discover the conversation too late may decide to pony up for access. According to Warner, his stream of new subscribers largely consists of "people coming to find [a particular] interviewee, and then joining the mailing list." When they join the list, they receive a few sample interviews and often become hooked.

Warner created *Mixergy* by trying to understand where he went wrong in his business. In the process of seeking answers, he's helped countless other entrepreneurs and built a recurring revenue stream for himself doing something he loves. "We have a couple of thousand people who are premium members at any given time," he says. "It's been working out really well." (For advice on another way to monetize quickly, see the sidebar "Launching a Crowdfunding Campaign.")

Develop an Online Community

Digital products like ebooks and all-access passes to virtual summits can be an excellent way to make money. But membership sites, which provide recurring revenue, add another layer. In a profession as uncertain as entrepreneurship, with its cycles of booms and busts, it's tremendously powerful to cultivate a consistent income stream. (Of course, people cancel or choose not to renew, but over time, those percentages can become predictable.)

With Warner's *Mixergy* site, people subscribe in order to access the vast archive of interviews and courses, enough to give yourself the equivalent of a college education if you consumed them all. But some entrepreneurs have discovered that another variation on a membership site can be even "stickier" when it comes to retaining members: an online community.

"They signed up for the information, and they stayed for the community": that's how Jason Van Orden describes the lesson he learned from running The Academy, a membership community he created focused on online marketing. Bjork Ostrom agrees. He and Lindsay created Food Blogger Pro, a community for food bloggers with eighteen hundred members. They feature more than three hundred videos on the site ranging from photography tips to technical advice about running a blog, with information about everything from WordPress to Google Analytics. But, he says, "In the long term, people stay because we have this forum of other people that are helping each other."

Smart businesspeople have long understood that it's easier to keep an existing customer than to win a new one. That's why building a membership site with recurring monthly or annual subscriptions works so well; it makes renewal simple—the default.

In a world where so much information is available online for free, it may seem surprising that people will actually pay good money (commonly in the $20 to $100 range per month) to join an online community. But active curation—an involved moderator setting the tenor of discussions and making sure they're both civil and useful—can make an online forum truly valuable.

Launching a Crowdfunding Campaign

When you've begun to assemble a following, another monetization option becomes available to you: crowdfunding. It's not the right answer for everyone, but it can provide a much-needed boost as you work to complete a project or activity. Here are tips from crowdfunding expert Clay Hebert, who has worked on more than 150 crowdfunding projects that have raised over $50 million, about how to get yours funded.

Build your own audience. Too many people assume that once their project is up on a crowdfunding site, funding will take care of itself. "You don't just throw up a Kickstarter campaign, and magically people browse Kickstarter and find you and give you money," says Hebert. "You need to build up an audience, a platform, and permission to launch your thing to them." If you don't already have a built-in audience, he suggests creating a landing page (a well-designed web page into which people can enter their email address) with a giveaway that people want, such as the first chapter of your book once it's written, or a helpful workbook or resource guide. He advised a client who was launching a high-end cat toy called the Kittyo to create a landing page through which people could register to win the toy. He found a niche site for cat lovers to partner with and generated two thousand email sign-ups in one weekend.

Start early. The Kittyo was a smash hit—fully funded in only thirty-six minutes after its launch, and ultimately raising $270,000—because its creator started his list-building efforts early. Through his landing page and giveaway contest, he had developed a list of 13,000 cat lovers who were eager to buy his product the moment the campaign went live. To a limited extent, you can rely on momentum to bring in revenue from people you don't already know, but you need to do most of the heavy lifting up front. In general, says Hebert, "You need to bring in the first 30 percent to 40 percent of crowdfunding yourself. You're launching to your tribe. Then if your project is interesting . . . those people are going to share it with the next ring, so that'll get you the next 30 percent or so, and then if you're 60 percent or 70 percent funded with two weeks to go, [generally] your campaign will be funded."

Think niche. Everyone would like to get their crowdfunding campaign featured on the national news or major business publications. Most likely, that won't happen. But even more interesting, it doesn't really matter, says Hebert. "Stop trying to get in the *Wall Street Journal*, and go to these little niche sites and blogs and little Facebook groups where people are passionate about your thing." A partnership that proved crucial for the Kittyo was with *Hauspanther*, which bills itself as "the premier online magazine for design-conscious cat people." That's a limited readership compared to the *Wall Street Journal*, but one that is perfectly suited for a high-end cat toy, in a way that generic business readers wouldn't be. Similarly, when Hebert advised a documentary filmmaker creating a movie about orphaned children of military veterans, he steered her to promote the campaign to military families by thinking carefully about the niche sites they frequented. Getting the right people to join your list is essential to your ultimate success. "You and I could build an email list by tomorrow of a thousand people if we did an iPad giveaway or an Apple Watch giveaway," says Hebert. "But those people won't then buy your book or [other product].

Find the best crowdfunding platform for you. Kickstarter, which focuses on creative projects, is perhaps the best-known crowdfunding site. But it's certainly not the only one. Examine each platform and evaluate its rules of engagement and where you'd have the greatest chance of success.

For instance, a few years back when I tried to create a Kickstarter campaign to fund a series of business advice videos, I was turned down before even launching because it wasn't deemed a "creative" enough project by their taste-making wizards (thanks, guys).

Busy with the launch of my first book, *Reinventing You*, I ultimately shelved the idea. But in retrospect, Indiegogo, which allows all kinds of projects—not just "creative" ones— might have been a better choice. It also offers the option of releasing pledged funds to the creator immediately or waiting until the campaign is fully funded. That's a key consideration given that more than 60 percent of Kickstarter campaigns fall short of their goals, meaning that their creators never collect a dime, even if they have thousands of dollars pledged.[6]

Keep in mind each site's policies about providing "rewards" to your supporters and what form that might take. Sending a digital album download is easy enough, but printing and mailing thousands of T-shirts (and getting the sizes right) can quickly become an onerous task that might make the whole enterprise less appealing. If you're doing rewards, you need to think them through carefully up front.

Besides Kickstarter and Indiegogo, among many others, Publishizer is a crowdfunding site focused on helping authors with preorders, and Patreon offers an interesting "recurring donation" model that may be especially helpful to those working to make a living from their art.

With Patreon, supporters don't make a onetime gift toward a specific project, like financing your indie film. Instead, they can opt in for an ongoing monthly donation to support your work in general (becoming a patron, as the site's name implies), or donate each time you create a piece of content. For instance, if I'm a fan of a certain podcaster's work, I could pledge $1 per episode, no hardship for most listeners, as you're getting an hour's worth of entertainment in exchange, and a way to give back to someone whose labors you've likely enjoyed for free in the past.

Over time, as you get to know the people who participate, you begin to develop real relationships. I've participated in online communities that host in-person meetings to foster connections, and I've referred business many times to colleagues I've initially gotten to know online. When your social and professional network becomes entwined with the online community you participate in, your membership stops being seen as discretionary. It's a necessity you can't live without.

Building a Community That Sticks

What does it take to build a cohesive, fee-based, online community? For one thing, it takes numbers. An online community with five people just won't have the volume or diversity of thought to create something useful. "When you start a paid community," says Canadian entrepreneur Scott Oldford, "I truly believe that you need not just twelve people or twenty-four people. In order to make it viable, it needs to be at least fifty members." So where do you get them?

Oldford suggests that launching a product or course is the perfect first step. Obviously, your buyers have a shared interest— in food blogging, online marketing, or whatever your product is. You can offer the online community as a way they can continue their learning. That's exactly the path Ryan Levesque took with participants in the online course he developed in 2014 focused on his survey methodology. He polled course participants to see if they might be interested in joining a paid online community after the class concluded; more than one hundred said yes.

He offered the early adopters a discounted subscription fee (half off the $100 regular monthly rate) and soon launched a private Facebook group and access to a private membership site featuring monthly training calls with both Levesque and a roster of special guest stars, lecturing on topics ranging from "how I built a seven-figure consulting business" to "ten daily changes I made in my life that tripled my productivity and doubled my income." Members also receive free access to Levesque's proprietary survey software.

In only two years, the community has ballooned from a hundred to more than two thousand members. In the process, Levesque has thought deeply about what makes for a desirable membership experience. "It's sort of like if you're involved in city planning," he says. "You can't just grow super quickly because there's infrastructure. There are highways, there's water supply, the things like that that need to grow with the growth of the community."

In a digital sense, infrastructure is about hiring the proper help to monitor the flow of conversation. "When the community first started, it was just me," says Levesque. "I was literally the community manager. I was in there on members' questions, supporting members, doing funnel reviews [in which he would evaluate members' work product]." But Levesque knew that couldn't last if the community scaled as he hoped it would. "With those first one hundred members, what I was keeping my eye out for were the superstars—people who were particularly engaged, people who were particularly supportive of other members in the community," he says.

What Levesque was looking for was a "community advocate," or someone who could serve as his proxy to keep the discussions positive, helpful, and productive. Levesque found a worthy candidate, hired him, and eventually promoted him to "community director," overseeing three new volunteer community advocates who received free membership in exchange for being helpful to other members and writing a weekly blog post. He soon realized, though, that even that arrangement wasn't sufficient. "We needed to make this a paid position," he said.

The stakes were high. Early members had become invested in the community, and they liked how it felt when it was small and intimate. Batches of newcomers brought new ideas and insights, but also shifted the social dynamic that had formed. "When you're introducing a hundred or two hundred members to the community all at once," says Levesque, "it can feel like, if you're not careful, a bunch of refugees coming in, where people have this kind of 'us vs. them' [feeling]."

After experimenting, he hit upon a ratio that felt right: one paid advocate for every four hundred group members. They've gotten deliberate about their processes, including how to bring on new members and ensuring there's a steady flow of introductory

Facebook messages, rather than a deluge as new people join. They've developed a sequence of private messages for new members, encouraging them to take one specific step with the community each day, such as reading a certain foundational blog post. The goal is to get them acclimated to the group and in the habit of participating.

Note that running an ongoing membership community can be an onerous job; Levesque's team just for this initiative now includes five advocates, a community director, and an administrative assistant. But, he says, it's worth it. "Is it worth having a business model where you're constantly having to support your customers, and constantly having to produce new content?" Levesque asks. "Well, the flip side to that is you get the best market intelligence that you could ask for, because your users, your audience, your tribe . . . they'll tell you. They say, 'Hey, here's what's missing. I wish you would do X.'" Having an active online community gives you the ability to survey your customers every day, so when you create a new product or service, you'll know for certain that they want it.

Try This:

If you like the idea of building an online community, ask yourself:

- Where will you get the initial members of your online community (at least fifty) from? Will you advertise it to members of your email list? Position it as the logical extension of a course or workshop that you've offered?

- What's your plan to stimulate conversation? What questions will you ask, and how often will you personally monitor exchanges? Plan a schedule for yourself in advance that reflects when you'll check in and what topics you'll ask questions about, so that community maintenance doesn't fall off your radar.

- Start thinking now about how you'll scale the community. After a certain point, you can't manage all the conversation and interactions yourself. Do you have someone who can help? Will you need to hire someone? Where will you find them? Promoting someone who is already a dedicated community member is often a good plan, but think now about your expectations of the role and compensation.

CHAPTER 11

Leverage Intellectual Property—Affiliate Marketing and Joint Ventures

When you have a big enough or targeted enough following, a new revenue option presents itself. You can begin to make money through affiliate relationships—basically, receiving a share of revenue in exchange for sending paying customers to a vendor.

This option can be lucrative, especially if you don't yet have a product of your own, but you do have a loyal audience. "You can create a great [web-based] product for less than $10,000," says Matt McWilliams, a joint venture expert. "But if you really have a small audience and you're like, 'I'm going to sell three of these,' it's not necessarily feasible to go out and spend, in many cases, $6,000 or $7,000 to create a product and invest dozens of hours of time." The better option is to promote other people's products instead, says McWilliams. "The barrier to entry is nothing."

Indeed, the very first affiliate promotion I ever participated in was an email I sent to the people on my list encouraging them to register for a $99 special webinar about networking hosted by McWilliams, John Corcoran, and another colleague of theirs. I knew the content would be good, so I felt comfortable recommending it. After sending dozens and dozens of emails over the years, I was astonished a few weeks later to receive a check for $365: my first sales commission. I had never directly earned money from sending an email before. It was an incredible feeling, and it made me realize the possibilities that I had, up until then, been neglecting.

This chapter will look at various aspects of affiliate relationships, from Amazon Associates and other company programs to relationships with other entrepreneurs (also known as joint ventures or JVs). We'll discuss how to organize large-scale JVs and how to find JV partners. Finally, we'll look at the nuts and bolts of partnering—including managing the process, making the commitment, and most importantly, maintaining your reputation.

Amazon Associates

The most well-known and ubiquitous affiliate program is probably Amazon Associates, run by the online retailer. If people click your link to enter Amazon's site, you'll receive a percentage (typically 4 percent to 8 percent) of anything they purchase within twenty-four hours. You can draw people to Amazon using helpful product links in blog posts, for instance. Lindsay

Ostrom of *Pinch of Yum* will write "pillar posts," meant to be definitive, in-depth articles about certain topics, such as preparing meals with slow cookers. She'll recommend certain brands, provide tips on using them effectively, and include relevant recipes. For each item mentioned, if Amazon sells it, she'll include a special link that will allow *Pinch of Yum* to earn affiliate income.

I typically earn between $100 and $300 per month from Amazon Associates—but it's a nice additional revenue stream that requires zero extra work. Some people, however, have done incredibly well with Amazon Associates; Darren Rowse of the website *Problogger* estimated that he earned more than $600,000 from the program over a thirteen-year period.[1]

Try This:

First, set up your Amazon Associates account (a quick web search will bring you to the right page). Now, consider the following:

- Think about products you can highlight (if you have a food blog, it might be slow cookers and kitchen supplies; if you have a business blog, it might be books or office supplies or certain types of software). What content can you create that will give you organic opportunities to present that item (such as an analysis of which slow cooker performs the best, or how using certain office supplies can improve your productivity)?

- To maintain trust with your readers, be sure to disclose when you're receiving affiliate income for recommending a product.

Affiliate Relationships with Other Companies

Amazon is an easy partner to work with because its brand is trusted and it sells a wide variety of items; you can point referral traffic to Amazon books one moment and to its cameras or fitness equipment the next. But its payouts are relatively low.

Other companies, however, have created affiliate programs that, when leveraged properly, can be quite lucrative for participants. Pat Flynn discovered this in 2010 when he launched a project he called the "Niche Site Duel," in which he and a friend both built websites from scratch focusing on industries in which they had no prior knowledge (Flynn chose security guard training). "We'd kind of compete to see who would be the first to make money, if it was even possible, and how much we could make overall," Flynn recalls. They'd chronicle their efforts publicly, sharing the good and the bad.

Flynn walked readers through his process of using keyword research tools to select his niche, and showed how he built the website that offered training for security guards, and began to attract traffic to it. With each step along the way, he was writing detailed blog posts and linking—with affiliate links—to the tools he was using. (See the sidebar "The Personal Side of Affiliate Marketing" to learn more about how to funnel more traffic to your affiliates.)

"Within seventy-three days, I was able to make my first dollar on that site," he recalls. The response from readers was immediate. "On the day that I shared that I was number one on Google [for security guard training] and I was making money, my affiliate earnings . . . went up by ten times. It was proof that what I was doing actually worked." To this day, a significant portion of Flynn's earnings come from affiliate arrangements with providers of the foundational business tools he recommends—the website hosting service BlueHost (more than $31,000 in March 2017 alone); the email service providers AWeber and ConvertKit (just under \$15,000 combined that month); and LeadPages, a tool that helps maximize your email subscriber acquisition (more than \$7,000 that month).[2]

Try This:

If there are influencers who you truly respect in your field, consider doing the following:

* Subscribe to their email list and see if they have courses or other products that they promote. (Buy them, so you can become even more familiar with their work.) If they do offer products, it's likely that they might offer an affiliate program. You can visit their website to look for more infor-mation or, even better, email them directly to inquire.

* If you're a passionate believer in the work they do—even if you only have a modest email list—they're likely to take note and respond. It's well known that fans make the best evangelists, because they can speak from their own expe-rience about how the influencer's products have helped them personally.

The Personal Side of Affiliate Marketing

When you recommend a product and send people to Ama-zon with your affiliate link, that can be a nice source of extra income. But affiliate marketing can also be a powerful form of networking and relationship building.

Selena Soo has mastered that principle. Although she sells her own products, like the "Get Known, Get Clients" course, Soo also serves as an affiliate for certain other online entrepreneurs. She's glad to earn the additional revenue, but that's not her main motivation. It's loyalty. "I've been affiliates mainly for two programs," she says. "One was for my mentor Ramit Sethi. The other was for my mentor Ryan Levesque. When it comes to stuff like that, I do get very competitive."

Soo views her ability to evangelize on behalf of her mentors as a way of connecting with them more deeply and showing her appreciation for their help. Recalling a promotion for a trial of Levesque's mastermind group, she says, "I remember just having this identity thing: I have to win. I cannot be number two. I'm not going to be able to live with myself . . . I want to show Ryan that I can do it."

Many people who agree to promote something might send a half-hearted, cut-and-paste email. But Soo was committed to making her message stand out. "That Friday evening," she recalls, "I sent an email to people—kind of a mysterious email to the whole list. I said to them, 'What if you could be part of a special VIP community where you could get personal feedback from the world's best entrepreneurs? I'm actually part of a special group like this that I rely on very heavily during my launches, and have helped me in all these high-impact ways. For a very limited time, they're opening up membership in this group, but it's invitation only and if you're interested, just reply to this email and let me know.'"

They were interested. Over the next forty-eight hours, eight hundred people emailed Soo back.

She didn't stop there, however. She offered free bonus material to her subscribers who signed up for Levesque's program—recordings of two webinars and a fifty-page PDF she'd created about the mechanics of her online course launch.

Her high-touch approach—citing her personal connection to Levesque, testifying to the benefits she'd received from the group, and offering extra inducements—worked perfectly. She drove 127 people to sign up for a trial membership in his group, winning the contest and a daylong, in-person retreat with Levesque. The money—just over $6,000—was incidental. "I got $50 per sale," she recalls. "That's a lot less than a $2,000 program, where you would typically get $1,000 commissions [in a JV arrangement]. I got a lot less, but it was more important for me to support my mentor."

Forming JV Partnerships

Affiliate relationships are often with companies, such as Amazon. But they can also be with other entrepreneurs, in JV partnerships. If you have a good relationship with someone and your products and focus area are aligned, entering into a JV can be a lucrative and mutually beneficial way to introduce each other to your respective audiences.

That's the premise of a private listserv that consultant Dov Gordon launched around 2009. It's called JVMM—Joint Venture Marketing Mastermind—and it brings together more than a hundred entrepreneurs who are interested in getting to know one another and potentially forming joint venture partnerships.

He had been looking for ways to market his consulting business, aimed at small businesses and entrepreneurs, but realized that traditional advertising was too expensive. Joint ventures with other entrepreneurs, on the other hand, seemed like an appealing prospect.

Here's an example of how joint ventures work. When I partnered with Gordon, I sent an email to my list promoting a free teleseminar he was conducting about how to improve the marketing process. I explained my connection with him, my respect for his work, and why readers might be interested. When any of my followers registered for his teleseminar, they were added to his email list (which they could choose to unsubscribe from at any point).

So, with one promotion from me or another partner, he could potentially add hundreds of emails to his list. "That's how you grow your list and how you grow your business," he says. The lack of upfront cost is an additional benefit. When Gordon started out, he says, "I was totally broke." But he didn't have to pay commissions to his JV partners unless a referral resulted in a sale and he himself got paid first. In our case, several of my readers signed on for consulting services with Gordon, earning more than $3,500 in affiliate commissions for me.

It all sounds good in theory, but Gordon says that JVMM wouldn't have worked unless he picked the right collaborators. He'd identified potential partners who served a similar audience and would subscribe to their emails, monitoring them over weeks or months to see if they'd be a good fit.

He ruled out professionals—even famous ones—if they didn't email their lists regularly or seem to promote other JV deals. And he also avoided those who embraced JVs but had a hype-filled, sales-oriented approach that didn't jibe with his style. For the right candidates, however, he'd eventually send out a brief message: "Hey, I've been on your list for a few months and I've been watching what you're doing. I think that you might qualify, or be a good fit for, this joint venture group," and then briefly explain it.

Now, nearly a decade in, the group almost always recruits new candidates from existing member referrals, but getting that initial mix right was critical to its success. Gordon was looking for collaborative players who were sharing their advice with everyone and were at least open to promote some members' projects if they aligned with their own focus.

The JV relationships Gordon has cultivated have been critical to his success. "It's been the main source of clients for our business," he says. "We've grown our list from a few hundred to over ten thousand."

Forming Large-Scale JV Partnerships

Gordon typically does one-off webinars with his partners throughout the year. But another form of JV partnership is to team up to promote a time-limited launch, which requires a huge amount of planning and coordination. That's where Matt McWilliams, who is also a member of Gordon's JVMM group, comes in.

His first foray into online marketing, he recalls, was rather disastrous. In the early 2000s, he cofounded a company that sold insurance leads, and he figured the internet would be a great place to find them. He spent more than $4,000 on banner ads and earned $8 in return. "Don't spend it all in one place," he says ruefully.

He clearly needed a better way. When he discovered affiliate marketing, like Gordon, he was drawn to the fact that you only paid if you actually generated sales: no more throwing away thousands of dollars with zero return. He eventually grew the company to more than $12 million a year in revenues and more than fifty employees, and developed substantial expertise in JV marketing in the process. Today, in a new venture, he manages affiliate relationships for authors and entrepreneurs like Brian Tracy, Lewis Howes, and Jeff Goins.

As Jeff Walker describes in his Product Launch Formula, the concept underpinning his popular eponymous online course, it's important to start with a seed or pilot launch, and to test the premise of your idea and see if people actually want to buy your product or service. Once that's validated, you can do what he calls an "internal launch"—releasing the product for sale to your own list, that is, the people who already like your work and trust you. Finally, as you gain more experience and know for sure that the product is both desirable and effective, you can launch it to a broader audience—the JV launch, which, if done right, can bring in hundreds of thousands or even millions of dollars.

Says McWilliams, "No matter how big your audience is—if you're Tony Robbins and you have a million people on your email list, or you're somebody just getting started out and you have five hundred . . . you have a finite number of books or products or whatever that you can sell on your own. There is a limit. There's no way to just expand that without involving other people."

Finding JV Partners

So, how can you find your own JV partners? Just as Gordon "stalked" potential JVMM members over time to determine if they'd be a good fit as partners, McWilliams and his associates do the same on an even larger scale. "Every single day, literally as you and I are talking right now, I have a team of virtual assistants who are scouring the internet," says McWilliams.

"We subscribe to pretty much every internet marketer's news-letter. We have a Gmail account that gets more than a thousand emails a day that is nothing but newsletters and marketing emails."

The goal is to see who's promoting what, and understand their overall style, tone, and interests. McWilliams starts by reaching out and introducing himself and perhaps offering some assistance with a launch they're doing. Over time, as they develop a rapport, McWilliams has a more direct ask: "Hey, we have a launch coming up with a client. Would you be interested in promoting it? Here's why I think it would be good for your audience."

You don't need to have McWilliams's volume of contacts (and team of virtual assistants to manage them) to find good JV part-ners, however. Referrals from friends and colleagues are usually the best way to find qualified contacts. And even if you don't have that, you can simply start Googling. McWilliams suggests searching for relevant terms in your niche, for instance, "guitar instruction affiliates." That enables you to build a database of relevant online marketers.

The best way to build relationships, if you're playing the long game, is "to reach out slowly and develop a relationship with them, follow them on Twitter, share their content," says McWilliams. Less desirable, but still workable, is reaching out with a direct ask for them to review or promote your course; some will still say yes.

Perhaps the best way to find affiliate partners, however, is actually becoming one yourself. "I think we've all been there with somebody in our life that we kind of look up to, and we send them an email or two and they never respond . . . I don't blame them, but it takes on a different thing when you make somebody money," he says. "When I promote somebody's launch, for example, and I do well and I make them $5,000 or $10,000 or $20,000," it activates their sense of reciprocity. They're far more likely to take an interest in your work, offer to be helpful, and perhaps even to become an affiliate for your products or courses, if your audiences are aligned.

Try This:

As you begin to look for possible JV partners, consider doing the following:

- Sign up for the email lists of others in your field. See whose approach resonates with you and who seems to participate in JV arrangements.

- Make a point of getting to know them over time. If you're going to be at the same conference, introduce yourself. Start following them on social media and sharing their posts. Reach out and offer to promote their products to your list, if appropriate. Over time, you'll have turned a cold contact into a mutually beneficial relationship.

Managing the Launch

Finding JV partners is only the first step, however. Once you've identified them, you need to provide them with the resources they need to successfully promote your work. This might include graphics or banner ads they could use, or sample copy for social media. But most important is the so-called "swipe copy"—sample emails they can use as a template to send to their audience, which explain who you are, what your offering is, and the benefits they'll receive by purchasing it. A typical launch period will last for several weeks, so this might include up to a dozen emails, though most launch partners won't send that many. "We suggest you edit it and put it in your own voice, but it's inspirational copy," says McWilliams. "It gives you the facts and the 'four bullet points this video is going to cover'–type stuff."

Providing your partners with sample copy and other resources is important, but it's not sufficient. "'Promote' has different definitions," says McWilliams. Someone might agree to support your launch and have the best of intentions, but if they have a busy week, they might send out one tweet and call it a day. Yes, they're losing possible affiliate revenue, but that's probably not their primary revenue source. But if it's your launch, having a partner essentially bail on his commitment can be a devastating setback and cost you thousands or tens of thousands of dollars. You have to keep them motivated and on track.

One common way to do so is publishing updated "leaderboards," which track the number of sign-ups and/or sales various partners have generated. That dynamic—the importance of being number one—certainly motivated Selena Soo in her quest to help Ryan Levesque's launch. "The reality is, most people in business are competitive," says McWilliams. Of course, if someone lets him know they dislike leaderboards, McWilliams will omit them, but in general, he's found them to be a motivating tool, often coupled with desirable prizes people can compete to win.

For example, I participated in one recent high-profile virtual summit in which the first prize was your choice of $10,000 or a Grand Canyon trip; second prize was a massage chair or $4,000; and third prize was a drone kit or $2,000, among others. Ultimately, however, few partners will agree to promote your work based on the chance to win a prize. Instead, their decision is based on respect for your work and the value that you can bring to their audience.

Indeed, for my first JV launch—partly because I had no idea how successful I would be and didn't want to overpromise—I eschewed leaderboards and prizes. My affiliates would receive a commission on any sales and my gratitude, but that was the only guarantee.

I still managed to sign up forty-two partners; the primary goal for most was simply to help me. I'd been an affiliate for some of them in the past, which is a great way to cement connections; others came through introductions from friends, or they'd reached out in the past to interview me for a blog or podcast. In order to protect the integrity of your launch and ensure people are motivated for the right reasons, it's best to start with your friends and your existing network, and build outward from there.

Making the Commitment

Another motivating tool, besides the leaderboard, is simply prompting people to make precommitments. McWilliams recalls his own experience promoting Danny Iny's launch. Instead of signing up every possible JV partner, Iny set a requirement: to participate in the launch, you had to agree to a detailed pre-call with him to discuss the launch strategy and lay out exactly when and how often you were going to promote.

The pre-call worked as a motivator, at least for McWilliams. During Iny's launch week, says McWilliams, he got tired late one Saturday afternoon. "I just wanted to be done working," he recalls. "It was the end of a long week, and I thought, 'You know what? I'm not going to write those emails for tomorrow. I'm done.'"

But then his conscience kicked in: "No, you told him you would mail nine times . . . You've only mailed six times. You need to write these emails." The resulting sales the next day earned McWilliams an extra $4,000, as well as a free trip to Atlanta to participate in a mastermind group with Iny. The reason he made the effort, he said, was "just that voice telling me, 'No, you committed to this.'" Now McWilliams ensures he has pre-calls with all his JV partners, as well.

Iny, who has studied launches extensively, explains his rationale. Typically, he says, "Over 80 percent or 90 percent of your results would come from your top five partners. My bias has always been that doesn't make sense. If that happens, it's because usually only the top five people on the leaderboard have their stuff together well enough to have done a good job. I was like, 'What if we help everyone do that well?'"

His first step was only approving partners who were all in on the launch. He turned away even those with a large list if they couldn't commit to focusing on the launch during its one to two weeks of peak activity. Iny spent up to an hour on Skype with each partner, going over the launch plan and asking them to mark down specific pledges about when and how they would mail to their list. "Putting in that extra effort, I spent forty hours of work, maybe a little more," he says. "That probably accounted for a million dollars in revenue."

Try This:

Before doing a JV launch of your own product, make sure you've been a JV partner for multiple other people, so you can get a sense of best practices and what approaches resonate with you. Take the time to plan exactly what you'd like your launch to look like. Ask yourself questions like:

- How many partners will I have?

- Who are they, exactly? (If you don't currently have strong relationships with these individuals, what will you do between now and the launch date to build a deeper connection?)

- What materials and swipe copy will you provide them, and by when?

- Will you hold a mandatory prep call? If so, what action plan will you recommend for them to best promote your work?

Maintaining Your Reputation

"Thanks for putting on a great webinar," the email read. "It was well organized and thought provoking. Gave me some ideas for expanding my business."

That was an appreciative message I received from a subscriber to my email list after doing a webinar with a JV partner. It's also a good example of what a successful partnership should yield—a positive impact on your followers. Unfortunately, that's not always what happens in JV partnerships, so it's important to be careful. After all, as an entrepreneur you can't put a price on your reputation; without it you've got nothing.

My own experience with JV partnerships began in the fall of 2015, when I experimented with hosting perhaps one or two a month on topics I thought would be of interest to my readers—networking, professional speaking, marketing strategies, and more. Some of these partnerships were spectacularly successful; a webinar with Iny promoting his online course earned me $11,000 in affiliate revenues in a mere two hours. Others were less effective, however, and ultimately weren't worthwhile if you consider the time needed to schedule, promote, coordinate, and host the webinar.

I collaborated with many different partners and, as McWilliams recommends, sought to learn the ropes before creating an online course of my own. I quickly noticed that there seemed to be a standard set of best practices. In the case of full-on product launches, I'd receive the swipe copy and sequencing information McWilliams described.

As I researched JV webinars more, I also discovered they seemed to have a typical presentation format. Often, it would begin with context setting, and the presenters explaining their own difficulties with the problem at hand (finding clients, networking, or the like). Then they'd explain how they solved it and how that solution changed their life, and they'd share information about their formula, before concluding with a pitch that those who were interested could take their learning further by registering for a course or consulting services.

In general, that's a solid format. After all, unless you explain why a problem is relevant to a customer and why you're the one to help, you're going to make few, if any, sales. But among shady internet marketers—the ones I strove to stay away from—things can be taken too far. Dov Gordon describes these presentation formats: "There's a lot of imitation, to the point where different people, they all start to sound the same."

The best webinars provide useful information and value to everyone who attends, even if they don't end up buying the product. But at the charlatan end of the spectrum, presenters often waste a huge amount of time at the beginning of the webinar with the setup of an archetypal struggle in which the hero describes his lowly state in detail—how he was broke and overweight and his marriage on the rocks—and then he was able to overcome it using magic secrets that he's about to unveil (but never actually seems to do). Throw in a healthy dose of wealth porn—pictures of him with his glorious house, family, car—and sketchy details about what his techniques actually entail, and you've created a ninety-minute teaser designed to infuriate savvy consumers and appeal to the lowest common denominator.

If you're partnering with such a presenter, your followers will associate that person with *you*. That's why I only agree to do JV webinars with practitioners I know personally, or who have been recommended by close colleagues. I always speak with them at length, review their materials, and make certain of their knowledge and abilities before agreeing to work with them. The reason I'm so careful is the same reason you should be: JV webinars, while relatively easy and potentially lucrative, also carry a harsh reputational risk if you choose the wrong partner to endorse, and your audience will hold you accountable.

Even with the safeguards I've put in place, however, I still received complaints about a couple of the partners I worked with. The same guy who earned me plaudits from the commenter I quoted earlier? His material was indeed excellent. But he turned out to be a fiend about email reminders, blasting those who had registered with endless follow-ups. As one attendee wrote to me: "While he has some valid ideas and clearly has built a successful business for himself, his high-pressure sales tactics and innumerable emails were a nuisance. Clearly I may be a minority and sales can be a numbers game . . . but tacky, tacky, tacky is the impression he left with me."

The vexing thing, when it comes to webinar best practices, is that the "tacky" techniques, whether in the webinar content itself or the follow-up, do seem to work surprisingly often. That can make it hard for even talented practitioners to resist them. After all, isn't following industry best practices what smart business people do?

Even so, what's missing too often is an understanding of the long-term damage that you can do to your brand. You might indeed sacrifice a few thousand dollars if you don't send the fifteenth email to your list reminding them that "the cart is closing now." But if you're intent on building multiple streams of income over the long term, rather than maximizing short-term revenues, you have to give up the ghost.

When it comes to schlocky sales tactics, says Gordon, "I skip that, and the reason I skip that is because I'm looking for certain kinds of [clients]. I don't know if it's the right thing to do or not. I don't know if I'd get a better result if I followed the same. I don't know and honestly, I don't care because it's a matter of how I want to be presenting myself."

To truly succeed—not just monetarily, but in terms of building a sustainable career and reputation for yourself—you need to cultivate a similar willful indifference, because you're playing a bigger game. That puts you in a great long-term position to enjoy the career and life you want. That's what I'll discuss in the final chapter.

Try This:

If you have an online course or product, start preparing your own JV webinar (plan for about an hour of content, including time for a brief sales pitch to explain your offering, and then an additional fifteen to twenty minutes of Q&A). Now, do the following:

- Test it out for your own audience first. How do people respond? How are sales? Once you've optimized it, you can think about offering it to other audiences.

- Make a list of potential JV partners who might like to have you present to their audiences. Ideal partners should be people you respect and have a good relationship with, and who speak to complementary audiences. It would be awkward to offer a webinar (and back-end course offering) on building a speaking career to the audience of a JV partner that does the exact same thing. But it could be highly lucrative to offer that person's audience a webinar about how to build your platform by writing a book, or how to create products to sell at your speaking events.

- Start with one to two partners with whom you have particularly strong relationships and agree to do reciprocal webinars (they present to your list, and vice versa). You won't always need to be reciprocal—sometimes their audience is a fit for you, but not vice versa—but it's a good way to start, and you can deepen your connection and work out the kinks with a trusted partner.

CHAPTER 12

Live the Life You Want

All entrepreneurs want to make money with the business they've created. But for many, the dollars are secondary. The real goal is freedom—the independence to live your life as you'd like, doing work you're passionate about and allocating your time to the things that matter most to you. But after years of growing a business to the point where you're in demand, you can find it hard to suddenly shift your priorities from gaining revenue and accepting every engagement to learning how to say no, so you can focus on aspects of the work you really love.

Michael Bungay Stanier faced just that conundrum. He's the Toronto-based entrepreneur mentioned earlier in this book whose business, Box of Crayons, now trains managers how to effectively coach their employees. Although he started out by coaching executives directly, he recalls, "At a certain point, I came to this insight that I actually didn't enjoy coaching that much." He was interested in helping people change behavior, but "it was too lonely, too isolated, the energy wasn't right." Even though he was finally making good money as a coach, he realized he needed to turn down that work in order to build a more sustainable business model that better suited his personality.

Similarly, for Jayson Gaignard, the organizer of the popular Mastermind Talks conference, it seemed like a no-brainer to start an even more exclusive, high-end mastermind group. He decided to bring together a group of professionals for quarterly, three-day retreats that were, in Gaignard's words, "really cool, once-in-a-lifetime experiences." Each retreat began with an "experience" day that featured an interesting activity to facilitate group bonding—such as behind-the-scenes tours of Cirque du Soleil, Apple University on the Apple campus, and the Aria Casino.

Day two of each session was a mastermind day in which participants could share their business challenges and learn from each other, and day three was a learning day, in which Gaignard would bring in outside expert speakers. Especially given the elite price point ($25,000 per person, per year), what's not to love?

But Gaignard found that, in contrast to his Mastermind Talks conference—which were tiring yet exhilarating for him—facilitating the retreats was merely exhausting. "It just didn't light me up. It actually drained me," he says. "I thought I'd enjoy it, but I realized I didn't." Despite hundreds of thousands of dollars in forgone revenue, he shut the program down after two years. Sometimes, to preserve your happiness, you have to say no to the money.

One strategy that makes this far easier is a commitment to keeping your overall expenses low, so you're never forced to do things for the money. The truth is, working to become a recognized expert and build a successful business takes time, and for a while, it *is* a zero-sum game. The time you invest in long-term growth is time taken away from short-term, revenue-generating activities.

My gross income dipped nearly $120,000 between 2011 and 2012 as I focused on platform-building activities and turned away business that would have kept me stuck in the old paradigm. My income rebounded a bit the following year, when my first book was released, but didn't come back fully until 2014.

I'm now making far more money than I was at my earlier peak in 2011, but many people wouldn't be willing to trade the guaranteed short-term payday, even if they're stuck in an ultimately unfulfilling business model, for the possibility of long-term gain.

Some have locked themselves into situations that make this difficult, including the golden handcuffs of pricey mortgages (I deliberately bought a condo in an "emerging" neighborhood as I was building my business, so I could live affordably and not stress out as much if my business had a setback). But if you have the ability to cut back strategically, I recommend it.

Spending less allows you more freedom to experiment in your business and, critically, room to pursue projects that are valuable but lack a short-term ROI. I now make a significant portion of my annual income from professional speaking—a location-independent business, as I fly to conferences and client sites to deliver my talks.

That wouldn't have been possible without focusing on blogging to build my platform, for which I received little if any money, and publishing my books, which put me on the radar of meeting organizers and executives that I would never have been able to connect with through my previous, referral-based growth model.

In this, the concluding chapter of the book, we'll look at ways to use the freedom you've gained as a *monetized* entrepreneur to truly create the life you want to live. We'll start by examining the pros and cons of growth, and then explore things like hiring a virtual assistant; getting other kinds of help you might need; deciding what kind of business you really want; reaping the rewards of travel; exercising your freedom of choice; and managing your time. I conclude with a reflection on why we work and how to get clear about what you're really working for.

Try This:

As you think about what kind of business you'd like to build, and the way you want to structure your life, ask yourself:

- What aspects of your business—not just administrative tasks, but core business functions—do you dislike the most? What would it take for you to move out of that business and transition into new revenue streams instead?

- What expenses can you cut without too much hardship? (The goal isn't to live an ascetic life, but to give you more flexibility in your business.)

The Pros and Cons of Growth

Our culture lionizes business growth—the Richard Bransons of the world with sprawling, multibillion-dollar empires. Depending on your goals, growth may be exactly what you need to focus on. That was Derek Halpern's approach.

He started his current business—the marketing and psychology website, Social Triggers—as a "solopreneur" with a laptop. When he started making some money, he took on an employee. By the time I interviewed him for this book, he had more than a dozen. "At this point, you start to realize the importance of continued growth," he says. "You also start to realize the importance of the fact that if you mess this up, fifteen people's lives are going to change, not just your own. I'm very big on going all in and taking risks, but I want to make sure that if one of my risks doesn't pan out for me, I don't sacrifice fifteen employees' livelihoods."

I experienced a small sliver of that feeling more than a decade ago, before launching my consulting business, when I was running a small bicycling advocacy nonprofit. I'd worked in more overtly high-pressure jobs before that; it's hard to beat running press on a presidential campaign and being awakened in the night by reporters' urgent phone calls.

But at an existential level, running the nonprofit was by far the most stressful. I had employees and a payroll, and a board that knew little about fund-raising. If the organization was going to stay afloat, it was on me to figure out how to bring it in. "What keeps you up at night?" has become a clichéd business question to elicit customers' pain points. But I literally woke up in the middle of the night trying to figure out how to bring in donations or service revenue to pay my employees.

When I left the nonprofit after two years at the helm, some people thought the move was risky. Entrepreneurship can seem extraordinarily daring to believers in the myth of a steady pay-check (having been laid off from my first job, I had no illusions left about that). But to me, becoming a solo consultant actually felt far less risky. I had been living on a meager nonprofit salary, and I knew, one way or another, I could figure out how to take on freelance jobs to support myself at the same level or even better. But perhaps the greatest benefit was the freedom I felt when I was no longer responsible for Jessie, Vance, or Mike. I vowed that I'd never take on a full-time, in-house employee again, and in more than a decade, I haven't.

Hiring a Virtual Assistant

But that pledge has also cost me on the flip side. About a year after starting my business, in 2007, I was busy enough, and earning enough revenue, to think about getting help. But I was hesitant to outsource any aspects of my business, so I started plowing money into part-time household help. I hired housecleaners, people to prepare meals for me, and assistants who could perform domestic chores like laundry. That was helpful, and freed up my time to focus on work. But I still needed help there and was too slow to realize it.

Not until 2013, seven years after I'd started my business, did I face the inevitable: I couldn't keep up. Before then, I'd managed to keep my clients happy, clean out my inbox almost every day, and make progress on a few key tasks—like writing my first book, *Reinventing You*—that moved my career forward. But with the book's release, I faced a wave of interview requests, speaking invitations, social media chatter, and general correspondence that I literally couldn't handle. My inbox swelled to hundreds of unanswered messages, and I ignored important requests for far too long. I felt a growing sense of panic, but simply didn't have time to fix the problem amid a grueling travel schedule and heavy client load.

I longed for help, but a previous, brief foray into trying out virtual assistants (VAs) from India had only lasted a week;

the company's definition of "English speaking" was a little too generous, and I knew that if someone were to represent me, they had to be able to communicate well in a professional context.

But when I found myself standing in line at a conference next to the executive director of a writers' organization—Eve Bridburg, later a case study in my book *Stand Out*—inspiration struck. Where could I find excellent writers who might need some extra money? Fiction authors! I asked Bridburg if she knew anyone who might be interested in working with me as a VA, and she offered to post a job notice on her group's listserv. Within a few weeks, I had hired Sue Williams, a talented writer and entrepreneur who has been working with me part time ever since on social media, basic web maintenance, and more.

I've also tried other configurations at times, including working with an enthusiastic Filipino VA. The upside of outsourcing to another country, of course, is that prices are much lower—$400 to $800 per month for a full-time employee in the Philippines is not uncommon. But you'll likely have to build in extra up-front training time and supervision, as you can't count on the same implicit assumptions that you'd share with someone from your own culture. And while it's certainly possible to find people who speak and write your language well, you may have to look carefully. An entire industry has sprung up to help you find and vet foreign VA candidates, typically charging around $500 to identify a pool of three to six candidates, from which you choose and then independently contract with them.

Getting the Help You Need

Whatever path you choose—domestic VAs, foreign VAs, or other forms of assistance—think through your desired staffing arrangements early on, before (as in my case) it becomes an emergency. When Bjork Ostrom of *Pinch of Yum* thinks about his business regrets, one comes immediately to mind. "I would've tried to build a team faster," he says. "We were trying to do all this stuff on our own." In the early days, it may be worth it to scrimp and plow the money you save back into the business. It also provides an important opportunity to learn about every aspect of the business, so you know in detail how it works and can later supervise others effectively. But knowing when to offload certain tasks is critical.

The Ostroms hired a bookkeeper and a certified public accountant to help with the financial aspects of their business. But Bjork has a broader wish list: he plans to hire additional people to help with administrative tasks such as customer support and answering emails. He knows his company's lack of staffing is hindering growth. "There's all these other areas where we're the bottleneck," he says. And he rues the company's lack of paid advertising heretofore: "That's a huge market that we could be reaching out into and I know that . . . if we had somebody on our team that could do that, it would be a huge multiplier for us."

Stefanie O'Connell, the millennial personal finance expert, agrees. Recently, she's been focused on hiring staff. "I can't continue to do a lot of the things that I've been doing personally," she says. But, while she's thrilled to have brought on an assistant, her vision of hiring help isn't just about outsourcing administrative tasks. She's hired a well-connected, high-end coach to help her develop her business and her brand. "I pay a lot of money for that," she says, "but to me, it's money very, very well spent. It's an introduction to media, to other brands. It's how I got my agent. It's been great."

Try This:

If you think you could benefit from some additional help, start by doing this:

- For two weeks, write down every business activity you do that takes at least fifteen minutes. Now make a chart. Where are you spending the most time? Which of these activities are core to your business (things you enjoy and only you can do)? Which are nonessential and can be out-sourced?

- Think about what skills you'd want in a VA, based on the tasks you need accomplished. If there's a lot of writing involved, you'll likely want a native English speaker. If you need technical help, such as podcast or video editing, you'll need to look for VAs with special skills.

- Once you have your job description finalized, you can either hire an agency to help you find candidates (con-sider this useful if you're hiring domestically and man-datory if you're hiring overseas), or you can identify candidates yourself (posting an ad on Craigslist, asking friends, or mentioning the job opening to readers of your own email list).

What Kind of Business Do You Want?

All businesses thrive on growth, but the question is, how much? Most people could probably benefit from a part-time assistant or outsourcing their tax preparation. But it's important to consider the ramifications of a growth model like Derek Halpern pursued. He's very successful, but he's not exactly lounging on a beach every day. When he started, he'd hustle to get any new subscriber to his email list that he could. If he thought creating a video or blog post could net him fifty new names, he'd do it.

These days, with more than two hundred thousand people on his email list, it's a different story. He says, "I can't be doing things that add a hundred people to my list anymore . . . Now I try to think up ways to add thousands of people to my list, tens of thousands of people to my list." That forces him to look for home runs, like a recent successful initiative in which his team, at a cost of nearly $25,000, developed an online "entrepreneur assessment test" that people could register to take in exchange for opting in to his newsletter. That effort brought him more than twenty-one thousand new subscribers in only four months, but not every gambit works as well. "There's been times where I spent tens of thousands of dollars to build something, launch it, and it ends up being a complete flop," he says.

When you run a business with salaried employees, the stakes for each move are much higher, and Halpern feels it. "When you have fifteen people as employees, the cost of building things goes up dramatically," he says. "Now we're trying to do a little bit more of a pare-down approach to try and limit costs of production . . . without blowing twenty or thirty or fifty or sixty grand before we actually figure out if it works. That's the focus. We try to create a big hit."

Contrast a business like Halpern's to what is sometimes called a "lifestyle business"—which has sometimes taken on a pejorative cast in the business world. As opposed to "real" entrepreneurs who seek to create scalable ventures that enjoy explosive growth and will earn investors a handsome profit, venture capitalists would never want to fund a lifestyle business. After all, there will never be an initial public offering or a leveraged buyout, but that's not the goal for this class of entrepreneurs. Instead, the focus of a lifestyle business is, quite simply, to provide its owner with an enviable quality of life. That often means a mix of priorities, both financial and personal.

That's how Jenny Blake, author of *Pivot*, thinks about her business. "At the end of the day, I love having space and quiet and time to travel and think and write," she says. "I have goals to earn a million dollars a year. I just wonder, does it need to happen with twenty employees, or can I do something like that on my own?"

As she points out, you have to get clear on what's important to you. "I've seen what people do to make seven figures," she says, "and I don't necessarily enjoy the same activities. So I've sort of taken the slower, more winding path that feels authentic to me . . . I leave every day around two or three to go to yoga; I don't work all day. I read for an hour in the morning. These are things I love doing and I'd rather have a slower-building income and keep a really healthy, calm lifestyle as much as I can."

Reaping the Benefits with Travel

Travel is a dream for many professionals, especially in the United States, where we're used to a meager two weeks of vacation per year, making it almost impossible to visit more distant locations like Asia and Australia. A chance to live in another country or to travel frequently often seems like a pipe dream. But if you follow the steps throughout this book and develop multiple income streams, it's not at all impossible to create a business that you can operate from anywhere in the world.

"In January of 2013," Blake recalls, "I wanted to go for two months to Bali and Thailand and try to work, but I was very nervous about that. I thought that maybe my business would go into a halt and wouldn't be recoverable—that I'd lose momentum and lose my clients and be done."

But she desperately wanted to try, so she booked her ticket. That month, it turned out, "I got the most coaching clients in the history of my business," she recalls. "I had a full book of business. We did have to deal with some Skype and internet glitches, but people were interested in how to do that [live abroad for two months] and they respected the courage to go do that." She even began to land a new client base of Australians, who were suddenly able to access her coaching appointments since their time zones now aligned.

Blake's sabbatical overseas, which she repeated two years later, is unusual in practice but a common fantasy. Natalie Sisson, however, has taken location independence to an extreme. For six years, she lived essentially without a fixed address, alighting for a month or two at a time in various destinations. She'd spent eight years working in the corporate world, but she wasn't fully content. "I'd like to travel the world," she thought to herself, "and I'd like to bring a business with me. How can I make this happen?"

She's visited sixty-nine countries, most of them during her six years on the road, and along the way lived in Buenos Aires, Amsterdam, Barcelona, Berlin, Los Angeles, and more. She makes her living from an assortment of activities, all of which she can handle from the road, including her online "Freedom Plan" course; an online membership program for entrepreneurs, the Freedom Collective; her book, *The Suitcase Entrepreneur*; speaking engagements; affiliate marketing; high-end coaching; as well as in-person workshops and retreats during her travels. (Test your own mettle for a life on the road in the sidebar "Are You Ready for a Location-Independent Lifestyle?")

Are You Ready for a
Location-Independent Lifestyle?

Working from beaches and traveling the world may sound appealing. But a location-independent lifestyle isn't for everyone. Here are some strategies and questions to help you determine if it suits you.

Try a travel pilot. You don't have to immediately sell all your belongings and hit the road. Jenny Blake recommends piloting both your overall enjoyment of travel and the particular location you're thinking about. She initially visited Bali for only two days, but she loved it. "It was all about yoga and spirituality," she says. "It was totally my scene." Her next trip was for a month, but she knew she'd enjoy it. "You don't have to move there for a year, cold turkey," she says. "Maybe you take a couple of trips in the next year."

Get your business ready. Even taking a few weeks off might sound like an impossible challenge. That's certainly true if you tried to plan something for next month. But when I took a month off to visit India in the fall of 2011, I notified my clients nearly a year in advance. There was plenty of time to strategize around my absence, and I made sure to put backup plans into place, including scheduling a month of social media posts in advance and determining which colleagues would cover for me if clients needed assistance. If you're planning to work part time or full time during your travels, this process may be relatively simple; during my trip, I completely unplugged so had to plan extensively in case problems arose.

Decide how much structure you need. On the road, no one is going to be looking over your shoulder and keeping you on task. "If you're good at managing your own time and you're productive and have discipline, you'll be able to do it [work] from anywhere," says Natalie Sisson. "But if you need to be in one place, and you need to go into an office, or you need to be surrounded by the same people all the time, it probably won't work for you." Understanding how you work best is an essential first step.

Determine how flexible you are. For better or worse, travel is unpredictable. Inevitably, you'll face canceled flights, hotel reservations gone awry, spotty Wi-Fi, and more. Sometimes that can lead to great adventures, but only if you aren't so frustrated and resentful that you can't get past it. "If you always like things to be 'just so,' if you like infrastructure to be there for you, it's probably not going to suit you," says Sisson. "Tropical islands always sound so great, don't they? But they're usually humid; there's mosquitos. There's always other things you don't think about."

Freedom of Choice

The flexibility of Sisson's career has paid off in more than one way. In August 2015, Sisson's father got sick, and she decided to move home to New Zealand to spend time with him. "That was the time at which I realized this freedom business model that I'd built actually gave me freedom in a totally different way than I tend to think about," she says, "which was to drop everything and come home to be with family. Had I still been in the corporate world, I wouldn't have had the leave; I probably wouldn't have had the time or the money to fly all the way home."

Her definition of freedom changed. It became, she said, "freedom of choice, and decisions, and what you make and how you spend your time. It became extra important to me during that time." Her father died that December.[1]

Sisson isn't the only successful entrepreneur who has used the freedom her profession affords to spend more time with family. Pat Flynn, whose *Smart Passive Income* empire brings in well over a million dollars a year, makes a point of mentioning his family frequently on his show and allocating his time to prioritize those relationships, including picking up and dropping off his kids at school every day.

"My business is structured around my wife, my kids, and my family, so actually, when they're awake, I'm not doing business," he told me. "I do business in the morning, before they wake up, during naptime like right now, or when they're in school." He says that hyper-focus on what matters has enabled him to be far more efficient in his business. If he ends up wasting time on Facebook, "I feel terrible about it, because I feel like that time was actually time not taken away from me doing my business, but from my children."

Flynn acknowledges the trade-offs he's made. "I've had a lot of opportunities to build bigger businesses, to make a lot more money, but it's very easy for me to say no to those things right now, because those things would get in the way of my priorities of being a father and being involved in their lives." His priorities and decisions might shift as his kids get older, but for now, maximizing the physical time he spends with them is paramount.

Try This:

When thinking about the level of freedom you want in your life and work, start by getting clear on your priorities—not what you think you should be aiming for, but what actually matters most to you. Ask yourself:

- Is your top priority spending time with your kids? Freedom to travel the world? Growing a seven-figure business? Doing yoga every afternoon?

- Write down, in detail, a description of your ideal day. How would you spend your time? Where would you be? Who are you with? Work backward from there. Knowing your end goal can help you determine how much money you need to facilitate your ideal lifestyle and the options available to you (if your top priority is making time for afternoon yoga classes, it's a lot easier to do that when you're a solopreneur, rather than running a hundred-person company).

Managing Your Time

For a while, as an entrepreneur, you have to learn to do it all. You start by cutting out the fat in your schedule—the trips down the Facebook rabbit hole, or the late-night TV watching, or even a certain amount of socializing. But before long, you've cut everything that's possible out of your day, and there's still not enough time. So you hire a VA or some staff, which frees up your schedule to concentrate on the most important tasks, and you find there's still not enough time. That's the price of success.

In today's fast-moving society, the amount of work—and not just busywork, but legitimately important projects or opportunities—will expand indefinitely to fill, and overflow, the time you have available. It's painful to say no, to disappoint others or even to turn down revenue. But if you're clear on your priorities, like Flynn's desire to spend time with his family, you can look to your North Star for guidance: Will this help me achieve my goal?

You also need to develop the discipline to focus on your most important tasks—the ones that can advance your business or your career, and often require extended, long-term effort. This is what Georgetown professor Cal Newport calls "deep work" (also the name of his book on the topic), and lies in contrast to "shallow work," that is, the quick-hit gratification of answering emails or completing low-end tasks. Doing that might keep you from getting fired, Newport says, but only deep work will enable you to get noticed, get promoted, and make a name for yourself.[2]

"The first year you're in entrepreneurship," says Antonio Centeno of *Real Men, Real Style*, "I think it's OK to work seventy, eighty hours a week. After that first year, I think you need to scale it down to forty hours," because that's what can make it sustainable for you personally over the long term.

The problem is, especially when you work for yourself, work can easily bleed in around the edges and you find yourself thinking, *Why not answer that email from your smartphone? Why not take that call on your writing day, just this once?* Centeno's strategy is to block out time on his calendar and hold it sacred. Tuesday and Thursday mornings, he takes his kids to the YMCA, where they have childcare while he works out, and then they go shopping together. He's also started taking Fridays off as a personal day. "By limiting that window [of available work time] to forty hours or even less than forty hours, it really forces you to cut off what's not important," he says. "I wish I would have done this a lot earlier."

Putting that discipline into his schedule wasn't easy. "I used to answer my phone all the time," Centeno says. "It could be a sale!" But now he funnels calls and meetings into specific blocks in his calendar. "If you're not my sister and you're not related to me or a deep personal friend . . . you're just going to have to wait," he says.

In those early, insecure days of entrepreneurship when you're scraping by to get every sale and make payroll, you may need to take every meeting or every phone call. But over time, you can begin to scale back strategically. "It used to be, I had all of Tuesdays and Thursdays completely open for meetings," recalls Centeno. "Before that, it was any days open." Now, he only takes meetings on Wednesday afternoons, so he's able to focus the rest of his time on high-impact activities.

Centeno's strategy of minimizing meetings and phone conversations reflects the philosophy that Paul Graham, founder of the startup accelerator Y Combinator, famously articulated in his essay, "Maker's Schedule, Manager's Schedule."[3] As Graham describes, managers—whose job is to supervise and motivate their employees—need to have days filled with short, staccato meetings. That's how they track their charges' progress and troubleshoot looming problems.

But "makers"—the people who are actually creating something—require something very different. They need uninterrupted blocks of time in which to let their creativity flow, unfettered. Even one or two meetings throughout the course of the day can disrupt their ability to immerse themselves in their work and accomplish their most important tasks. For managers, a day full of meetings is a productive one. For a maker, a day full of meetings is almost always a waste.

When you're an entrepreneur—and especially once you've gained some success—people covet your time. Your employees seek supervision and guidance. Potential partners want to brainstorm deals. Bloggers want to profile you, and podcasters want to interview you. And—inescapably—old friends and friends-of-friends want to pick your brain.

Some of these meetings are wise investments. They might lead to new revenue streams or business deals, or deposits in the favor bank that can be cashed in at an auspicious time. But having too many of them will destroy you. Perhaps, once you've built out your empire, you'll have ghostwriters to author your books; education consultants to create your online courses; and directors of strategic partnerships to handle your networking and relationship building. But for a very long time—perhaps forever—those high-value tasks need to be completed *by you*. If you fail to make time for them and let the pressing exigencies of "shallow work" define your schedule, you'll fail to do what matters most.

Personally, I make sure I accomplish my high-value tasks by sharply limiting the number of projects I focus on each year. Every six months, I identify two primary professional goals; everything else, unless it directly makes me money or is a mandatory administrative task, gets shunted aside. For instance, in the first half of 2015, my goals were to successfully launch my previous book, *Stand Out*, and to work toward doubling my email list to twenty thousand by the end of the year. In the latter half of the year, I continued my focus on email list growth (I eventually increased it to twenty-five thousand by the end of the year), and shifted to a new literary goal, which was finalizing the proposal for this book and getting it sold.

As the saying goes, people tend to overestimate what they can accomplish in a day and underestimate what they can accomplish in a year. By choosing only two major goals at a time, I force myself to make progress by concentrating my efforts. As someone with a lot of interests, it pains me to limit myself. In my dream world, I'd like to simultaneously start a podcast, write a book, create a video series, and do a JV online course launch. But that would be a mistake, because I couldn't do any of them well.

The point of this book isn't that you should be trying every single strategy, and certainly not at the same time. You might find YouTube videos annoying, or dislike coaching, or scorn the concept of an online course. All that is fine.

The point is to present you with a smorgasbord of options. No one can, or should, do everything, because you can't do everything well. Instead, you should find the activities that interest and delight you, and enable you to leverage the work you're already doing. Feel free to experiment and sample and pilot; it's often impossible to know what will appeal to you before you try it. But once you find an avenue you enjoy, double-down and work on mastering it before adding on another activity. "Deep work" is what will get you recognized, attract an audience, and allow you to monetize your ideas.

When it comes to becoming a successful entrepreneur and building up multiple revenue streams, whether or not you ever plan to leave your day job, what matters most is *focus and execution*. The time won't open up on its own. You have to forcibly make room in your schedule to write that blog post, record that podcast, attend that conference, or create that curriculum. But when you make it a priority and a habit, amazing things start to happen.

Try This:

Effective time management is the secret to making your intentions real. Ask yourself:

- What two—and only two—activities will you focus on in the next six months? Write them down, and break them into smaller pieces. What can you do today, and this week, to move the ball forward?

What Are You Working For?

As we know all too well, change has come to the world of work, and it will surely continue. In the 2000s, change disrupted the newspaper world just when I had decided I'd like to be a journalist for the rest of my life. We don't know what industries will be disrupted next. We see glimmers of the future—artificial intelligence, virtual reality, self-driving cars, and 3D printing are sure to be major forces. But what companies and industries will rise and fall accordingly? And will the shakeout take five years, or twenty-five? It makes a profound difference in your career arc, yet none of us can know with certainty.

Productivity Resources

You can download a free list of the tools and resources I use to stay productive at dorieclark.com/productivity.

All we can do is prepare ourselves to seize opportunities, to be ready to apply our knowledge and skills in new ways. I've always loved writing, and today, I'm still a journalist of sorts. I write books and blog posts, and though the compensation is low, it enables me to make money in other ways, attracting lucrative consulting and speaking business. And it draws in individual readers who might join my email list and eventually sign up for coaching services or participate in my workshops or online courses.

When I finished graduate school nearly twenty years ago, I couldn't have predicted the job I now have. The pieces I dreamed about are all there—reading, writing, sharing ideas—but the form is quite different. Frankly, it's better: more financially rewarding, more autonomous, more fulfilling. But I had to be willing to give up the ghost of what I had imagined, in order to grasp what was possible.

These days, the greatest job security possible comes from learning your craft, marshaling social proof, and developing multiple, sustainable revenue streams. When you're no longer reliant on one company or one form of income, you've rendered yourself disruption-proof. You've taken control.

It's not just about hedging your bets, of course. Figuring out how to monetize your expertise, in multiple ways, also allows you the freedom to determine what you really want your life to look like.

Before the advent of the internet, the options were relatively limited. Perhaps you could luck into a glamorous career as a novelist or overseas language teacher or high-end freelance consultant. But those opportunities were rare, and for the vast majority, supporting yourself meant going into an office every day, working nine to five (or worse) and contenting yourself with a meager allotment of vacation time.

But now, we're finally starting to reap the benefits that technology has promised. For those willing to adjust and pivot, the opportunities are boundless. Just because journalism jobs are gone doesn't mean you can't become a journalist. We're inventing our own categories now, and making even more money in new ways.

It's a time of panic and suffering for people insistent on clinging to the past. But if you're willing to think creatively about how to turn your knowledge and expertise into multiple revenue streams, you can create a diversified income with maximum freedom. Maybe it's freedom to travel the world, like Natalie Sisson. Or freedom to take an active role in raising your kids, like Pat Flynn. Or freedom to take extended vacations in places that speak to your soul, like Jenny Blake.

When my first book, *Reinventing You*, came out in 2013, I knew I had to capitalize on it. To accept every media interview or seize every speaking opportunity—that was an investment in my future. The more people knew about me and my work, I figured, the more success I'd have in the future. I was coming off a bad breakup, and especially after my beloved cat died, I didn't see a reason to stay at home; nothing felt like home. For three years, I spent almost all my time on the road, notching 194 separate speaking engagements. I was excited to see new places, enjoyed the occasional glamour of travel (in between its crushing indignities), and, frankly, welcomed the distraction from my personal life.

But eventually it was enough.

Speaking at conferences and events, and traveling to consult with clients, will always be part of my business model. But if you make your money exclusively from providing services, you're limited by time or your physical capacity. And after giving seventy-four talks in 2015 alone, I was hitting my limit. I just wanted to be home in New York, and I knew that creating new, internet-enabled revenue streams would allow me to do that.

Monetizing your ideas and embracing entrepreneurship means, quite simply, that you have more options. You can choose to stay in your day job, if you have one, knowing you have the safety of a backup plan. And if you go all in on working for yourself, you have the ability to refashion your life and your career as you see fit.

For several years, traveling almost nonstop was what I wanted; it was an exciting, high-intensity way to see the world and meet people I wouldn't otherwise have the chance to. Perhaps at some point, the frequent travel is something I'll want to return to. But just as Sisson—the "Suitcase Entrepreneur"—decided to return home to care for her ailing father, there are seasons in what we need and desire. I wanted to lessen my dependence on the road and begin to build a different kind of career and life for myself, with more time in New York. I wrote this book to learn, and share with others, how to expand my own options and build a career that's lucrative and flexible enough to allow me to live life on my own terms.

Your work life and your home life are ultimately the same thing. Sharing your best ideas with the world is a powerful way to help others and give meaning to what you do. But we've entered an era in which influence and revenue have become decoupled. Because anyone can blog or podcast or self-publish, content has often devolved into a commodity. In order to make your efforts sustainable, you have to think creatively and consciously about how to monetize your ideas. With this book, I've tried to present a road map for you to do just that.

The world needs your ideas—and you need to be paid for them. That's the path to lasting influence, impact, and freedom.

Self-Assessment Workbook

To continue the conversation, download your free copy of the *Entrepreneurial You* Self-Assessment Workbook. It includes all the "Try This" questions in this book in easy-to-print format, so you can write down your answers and get started on creating the lucrative and thriving career you deserve. Download it for free at dorieclark.com/entrepreneur.

NOTES

Chapter 1

1. Bozi Dar is a pen name. Bozi (his real first name) prefers to write books and teach his courses under a pseudonym in order to separate his corporate and entrepreneurial work.

2. Mary Meeker, "Internet Trends 2016—Code Conference," KPCB, June 1, 2016, slide 98, http://www.kpcb.com/internet-trends.

3. Nelson D. Schwartz, "U.S. Growth and Employment Data Tell Different Stories," *New York Times*, January 17, 2016, http://www.nytimes.com/2016/01/18/business/economy/us-growth-and-employment-data-tell-different-stories.html.

4. Carl Bialik, "Seven Careers in a Lifetime? Think Twice, Researchers Say," *Wall Street Journal*, September 4, 2010, http://www.wsj.com/articles/SB10001424052748704206804575468162805877990.

5. Amy Adkins, "Majority of U.S. Employees Not Engaged Despite Gains in 2014," Gallup, January 28, 2015, http://www.gallup.com/poll/181289/majority-employees-not-engaged-despite-gains-2014.aspx.

6. Jeffrey Sparshott, "By One Measure, Wages for Most U.S. Workers Peaked in 1972, *Wall Street Journal*, April 17, 2015, http://blogs.wsj.com/economics/2015/04/17/by-one-measure-wages-for-most-u-s-workers-peaked-in-1972/.

7. "Freelancing in America: 2015," Daniel J. Edelman Inc., September 24, 2015, http://www.slideshare.net/upwork/2015-us-freelancer-survey-53166722/1.

8. "Freelancers Union and Upwork Release New Study Revealing Insights into the Almost 54 Million People Freelancing in America," Upwork press release, October 1, 2015, https://www.upwork.com/press/2015/10/01/freelancers-union-and-upwork-release-new-study-revealing-insights-into-the-almost-54-million-people-freelancing-in-america/; Vivian Giang, "40 Percent of Americans Will Be Freelancers by 2020," *Business Insider*, March 21, 2013, http://www.businessinsider.com/americans-want-to-work-for-themselves-intuit-2013-3.

9. David Searls, "Adventures with Because Effects," *Doc Searls Weblog*, November 28, 2007, https://blogs.harvard.edu/doc/2007/11/28/ adventures-with-because-effects/.

Chapter 2

1. Nicholas Carlson, "Facebook Slightly Tweaked How The Site Works—And It Screwed An Entire Profession," *Business Insider*, December 13, 2013, http:// www.businessinsider.com/facebook-screws-social-media-marketers-2013-12.

2. Danny Sullivan, "Just Like Facebook, Twitter's New Impression Stats Suggest Few Followers See What's Tweeted," *Marketing Land*, July 11, 2014, http:// marketingland.com/facebook-twitter-impressions-90878.

3. "Email Statistics Report," 2015–2019, Radicati Group, February 2015, http:// www.radicati.com/wp/wp-content/uploads/2015/02/Email-Statistics-Report-2015- 2019-Executive-Summary.pdf.

Chapter 4

1. Libby Kane, "A woman who went from earning $42,000 a year to building a business that earns over 7 times as much shares her best advice for entrepreneurs," *Business Insider*, March 29, 2016, http://www.businessinsider.com/ selena-soo-best-advice-for-entrepreneurs-2016-3.

2. Tom Peters, "The Brand Called You," *Fast Company*, August 31, 1997, https://www.fastcompany.com/28905/brand-called-you.

Chapter 5

1. Dorie Clark, "How to Become a Successful Professional Speaker," *Forbes*, June 10, 2013, http://www.forbes.com/sites/dorieclark/2013/06/10/ how-to-become-a-successful-professional-speaker/#3e073b61326f.

2. Ibid.

Chapter 6

1. Josh Morgan, "How Podcasts Have Changed in Ten Years: By the Numbers," *Medium*, September 2, 2015, https://medium.com/@slowerdawn/how- podcasts-have-changed-in-ten-years-by-the-numbers-720a6e984e4e#.nnd438vtn.

2. "Connected Car Forecast: Global Connected Care Market to Grow Threefold Within Five Years," GSMA, April 2013, http://www.gsma.com/ connectedliving/wp-content/uploads/2013/06/cl_ma_forecast_06_13.pdf.

3. Dorie Clark, "Here's the Future of Podcasting," *Forbes*, November 19, 2014, http://www.forbes.com/sites/dorieclark/2014/11/19/ heres-the-future-of-podcasting/#7889ecfac7e6.

4. Morgan, "How Podcasts Have Changed in Ten Years: By the Numbers."

5. Steven Perberg, "Podcasts Face Advertising Hurdles," *Wall Street Journal*, February 18, 2016, https://www.wsj.com/articles/podcasts-face-advertising-hurdles-1455745492.

6. Ibid.

7. Hank Green, "The $1,000 CPM," *Medium*, April 5, 2015, https://medium.com/@hankgreen/the-1-000-cpm-f92717506a4b#.e26renkgh.

Chapter 7

1. "November Traffic and Income Report," *Pinch of Yum*, December 19, 2016, http://pinchofyum.com/november-traffic-income-report#income.

2. Clive Thompson, "The Early Years," *New York Magazine*, n.d., http://nymag.com/news/media/15971/.

3. Dan Schawbel, "Mario Forleo: How She Grew Her Brand to Oprah Status," *Forbes*, May 16, 2013, http://www.forbes.com/sites/danschawbel/2013/05/16/marie-forleo-how-she-grew-her-brand-to-oprah-status/#6335276d2135.

4. "Ultimate Guide to Double Monk Strap Dress Shoes," *Real Men, Real Style*, n.d., http://www.realmenrealstyle.com/guide-double-monk-strap/.

Chapter 9

1. Jared Kleinert, "Should Millennials Get Into Internet Marketing?" *Forbes*, December 7, 2015, http://www.forbes.com/sites/jaredkleinert/2015/12/07/should-millennials-get-into-internet-marketing/#7c76a724309d.

2. Pat Flynn, "SPI 190: Step by Step Production Creation with Bryan Harris," *Smart Passive Income*, December 2, 2015, http://www.smartpassiveincome.com/podcasts/spi-190-step-step-product-creation-bryan-harris/.

Chapter 10

1. Joanna Penn, "Six Figure Success Self-Publishing Non-Fiction Books With Steve Scott," *Creative Penn,* October 14, 2014, http://www.thecreativepenn.com/2014/10/14/non-fiction-success/.

2. James Altucher, "How to Go from $0–$40,000 a Month Writing From Home," July 2014, http://www.jamesaltucher.com/2014/07/ep-23-go-0-40000-month-writing-home/.

3. Steve Scott, "9 Steps for Building an Email List from Scratch," n.d., http://www.stevescottsite.com/new-email-list.

4. Tim Ferriss, "How a First-Time Author Got a 7-Figure Book Deal," The Tim Ferriss Show, April 15, 2013, http://fourhourworkweek.com/2013/04/15/how-to-get-a-book-deal/.

5. Alexis Grant, "Make a Living on Your Own Terms, Doing Work You Love," n.d., http://alexisgrant.com/self-employment/.

6. "Kickstarter vs. Indiegogo: Which One to Choose," The Crowdfunding Formula, n.d., https://thecrowdfundingformula.com/2015/11/13/kickstarter-vs-indiegogo-2/.

Chapter 11

1. Darren Rowse, "How I Started Making Money with Amazon's Affiliate Program," *ProBlogger*, April 24,2013, http://www.problogger.net/archives/2013/04/24the-ultimate-guide-to-making-money-with-the-amazon-affiliate-program/.
2. Pat Flynn, "My April 2016 Monthly Income Report," *Smart Passive Income*, May 9, 2016, http://www.smartpassiveincome.com/income-reports/my-april-2016-monthly-income-report/.

Chapter 12

1. Natalie Sisson, "Looking for More Freedom in Your Life? Here's How I Did It . . . ," *The Suitcase Entrepreneur*, http://suitcaseentrepreneur.com/about/.
2. Cal Newport, "Deep Work," *Art of Charm*, http://theartofcharm.com/podcast-episodes/cal-newport-deep-work-episode-515/.
3. Paul Graham, "Maker's Schedule, Manager's Schedule," July 2009, http://www.paulgraham.com/makersschedule.html.

INDEX

ACKNOWLEDGMENTS

I'm grateful to the many people who made *Entrepreneurial You* possible, starting with the talented entrepreneurs who shared their stories in these pages and have helped inspire so many others to build the careers and lives they want.

My agent, Carol Franco, capably guided this book, as well as *Reinventing You* and *Stand Out*, into the world. And I was delighted to be reunited with my *Reinventing You* team at HBR Press, including my editor Jeff Kehoe and Stephani Finks, who created the cool cover concept. Thanks also to publicity mavens Julie Devoll and Nina Nocciolino, editorial assistant Kenzie Travers, and production editor Dave Lievens.

Sue Williams has worked with me for more than four years, and her talent and digital savvy have helped me tremendously in my quest to be responsive to my readers and colleagues through the myriad of channels we face today.

Thank you to my wonderful readers, who have given me the opportunity to share my thoughts, and who have enriched me through our dialogue. I'd like to give a special shout-out to the students in my Recognized Expert course, who have accomplished so much and make me proud every day as they work to spread their own breakthrough ideas.

To join the more than 50,000 readers I'm in regular touch with, you can download the free *Entrepreneurial You* self-assessment at dorieclark.com/entrepreneur.

I'm also grateful to the many institutions that have invited me to write, speak, teach, and share ideas, from *Harvard Business Review* to Duke University's Fuqua School of Business, and beyond.

The foundation for accomplishing anything, especially an intensive and long-term project like writing a book, is having loving and supportive people in your life. I feel lucky every day to have a mother like Gail Clark, whose encouragement knows no bounds. I'm also grateful to Ann Thomas, who helped raise me with love and care, and Shoshana Lief, who helped me remember to enjoy life while in the midst of the book-creation process.

I'm appreciative to be part of such a talented community of friends, including but not limited to Jenny Blake, Joel Gagne, Alisa Cohn, Jessica Lipps, Rich Tafel, Jason and Melanie Van Orden, Marie Incontrera, Petra Kolber, Susan RoAne, John Corcoran, Jordan Harbinger and Jen Liao, Judah Pollack, Ben Michaelis, Kabir Sehgal, Jessi Hempel, Kaja Perina, Stephen Morrison, Ron Carucci, Shama Hyder, Micheal and Amy Port, many more. Patty Adelsberger is also never far from my mind.

No acknowledgments section would be complete without talking about cats, our greatest collaborators and interlocutors. Just around the time I finished the initial draft of *Entrepreneurial You*, I adopted two stray kittens, Heath and Phillip. They have brought immeasurable joy to my life, especially after the loss of my beloved cat Gideon and my cat daughter, Harriet. Adopting a homeless pet is one of the greatest things a human can do, and their love shows you how to become a better person. Visit petfinder.com or visit your local shelter to meet your feline or canine bashert today.

ABOUT THE AUTHOR

Dorie Clark is the author of *Reinventing You* and *Stand Out*, which was named the number one Leadership Book of 2015 by *Inc.* magazine, one of the Top 10 Business Books of the Year by *Forbes*, and was a *Washington Post* bestseller. A former presidential campaign spokeswoman, she teaches at Duke University's Fuqua School of Business. She is a frequent contributor to *Harvard Business Review* and is a consultant and speaker for clients such as Google, the Bill and Melinda Gates Foundation, and the World Bank. She is also a producer of a multiple Grammy-winning jazz album. You can download her free *Entrepreneurial You* self-assessment and learn more at dorieclark.com.